Evidence-Based Resources for Behavioral Health

The Dartmouth PRC–Hazelden imprint was formed as a partnership between the Dartmouth Psychiatric Research Center (PRC) and Hazelden Publishing, a division of the Hazelden Foundation—nonprofit leaders in the research and development of evidence-based resources for behavioral health. The internationally recognized Dartmouth PRC staff applies rigorous research protocols to develop effective interventions for practical application in behavioral health settings. Hazelden Publishing is the premier publisher of educational materials and up-to-date information for professionals and consumers in the fields of addiction treatment, prevention, criminal justice, and behavioral health.

Our mission is to create and publish a comprehensive, state-of-the-art line of professional resources—including curricula, books, multimedia tools, and staff-development training materials—to serve professionals treating people with mental health, addiction, and co-occurring disorders at every point along the continuum of care.

For more information about Dartmouth PRC–Hazelden and our collection of professional products, visit the Hazelden Behavioral Health Evolution Web site at www.bhevolution.org.

Dartmouth PRC | HAZELDEN®
Evidence-Based Resources for Behavioral Health

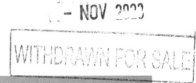
Severe Mental Illness Program

Supported Employment

Applying the Individual Placement and Support (IPS) Model to Help Clients Compete in the Workforce

UPDATED AND EXPANDED

Sarah J. Swanson

and

Deborah R. Becker

Hazelden
Center City, Minnesota 55012
hazelden.org

ISBN: 978-1-61649-085-0

Editor's note

Some names, details, and circumstances have been changed to protect the privacy of
those mentioned in this publication.

This publication is not intended as a substitute for the advice of health care
professionals.

Quotes from Andrea Wigfield, Becky, Claire Beck, Diane Erkens, father of client,
Jesse, Julie Cadwallader, Julie Temple, Kristin Tracy, Mark, Nicole Clevenger, Tania
Morawiec, and Ted are used with permission.

Cover design by David Spohn
Interior design and typesetting by Madeline Berglund

▼

CONTENTS

Duplicating this page is illegal. Do not copy this material without written permission from the publisher.

V

▼

PREFACE

This book is for employment specialists, IPS supported employment supervisors, vocational rehabilitation counselors, and mental health practitioners. We present the basic information and skills needed to deliver evidence-based supported employment. Family members and people with mental illnesses who want to learn about IPS supported employment services may also be interested in reading this manual. Supervisors and agency leaders will need additional information about setting up, organizing, and otherwise implementing and sustaining the program. A more comprehensive discussion of these broader issues is provided in Becker and Drake's *A Working Life for People with Severe Mental Illness* (2003). The Dartmouth Psychiatric Research Center's IPS Supported Employment Web site is another source for current information, program tools, demonstration videos, and fidelity materials (www.dartmouth.edu/~ips).

This book is divided into the following sections:

SECTION	CONTENT	AUDIENCE
SECTION 1 *Chapters 1–2*	Provides an overview of the evidence-based practice of IPS supported employment.	Applicable to any person wishing to know more about IPS supported employment, including mental health practitioners, family members, clients, medication prescribers, substance use counselors, vocational rehabilitation counselors, and employment specialists.
SECTION 2 *Chapters 3–9*	Describes the skills and practices of IPS practitioners.	Essential information for employment specialists and their supervisors.

continued on next page

SECTION	CONTENT	AUDIENCE
SECTION 3 *Chapters 10–13*	Explains how IPS uses a team approach. Defines the roles of mental health practitioners, family members, vocational rehabilitation counselors, and supervisors in the vocational process.	IPS supervisors will find each chapter helpful. Vocational rehabilitation counselors, family members, and mental health practitioners may be most interested in the chapter about their individual role in the process.
APPENDIX A *IPS Supported Employment Fidelity*	Introduces and provides an overview of the IPS fidelity scale, a vital tool to ensuring good services and sustaining superior outcomes.	Agency administrators and supervisors who oversee the IPS program will need to understand this material, but it is recommended for anyone interested in how IPS supported employment services are organized and provided.

The CD-ROM is divided into these parts:

SECTION	CONTENT	AUDIENCE
PART I *IPS Supported Employment Fidelity*	Provides the fidelity scale and score sheet, a sample fidelity action plan, and a sample fidelity report.	Agency administrators and supervisors who oversee the IPS program will need to understand this material, but it is recommended for anyone interested in how IPS supported employment services are organized and provided.
PART II *IPS Supported Employment Tools*	Provides a variety of tools, forms, and samples.	IPS supervisors and others who are responsible for establishing program practices will be interested in these tools.

Individual Placement and Support (IPS) supported employment is inclusive and uses a team approach. Note that the charts above outline which sections of this book are aimed at specific team members. However, we recommend that everyone involved in IPS supported employment read the entire book and review the material on the accompanying CD-ROM. Knowing the roles of other team members helps all members work together effectively.

In both this manual and the accompanying CD-ROM, we refer to the people who receive mental health and supported employment services as *clients*. Other terms, such as *consumers, service users, survivors,* and *patients* are used in different settings. We chose the term *client* because it is widely used by different stakeholders across many countries. Also, we use the term *severe mental illness* to refer to the approximately 5 percent of people who are disabled by severe mental illness.

Many programs across the United States and in other countries use the term *supported employment*. These programs may or may not be using the evidence-based approach. In this manual, we use the term *IPS supported employment* to differentiate the evidence-based practice for people with severe mental illness from other types of supported employment. *IPS* stands for *Individual Placement and Support*.

We thank the many practitioners, clients, family members, and employers whose experiences have increased our knowledge of how to support people with psychiatric disabilities in their work lives. This manual includes many of these experiences.

• • •

▼

HOW TO ACCESS THE RESOURCES ON THE CD-ROM

The *Supported Employment* CD-ROM contains electronic versions of the forms and handouts referred to in this manual. All of these resources are in PDF format and can be accessed using Adobe Reader. If you do not have Adobe Reader, you can download it for free at www.adobe.com.

Whenever you see this icon ⬜1 in this guide, this means the needed resource is on the CD-ROM. The number on the icon corresponds with the number of the document on the CD-ROM. Some of the resources on the CD-ROM are also available in Spanish. When you see this icon (SP), this means the needed resource is also in Spanish.

To access these resources, put the disk in your computer's CD-ROM player. Open your version of Adobe Reader. Then open the documents by finding them on your CD-ROM drive. These resources cannot be modified, but they may be printed for use without concern for copyright infringement.

See page 223 for a list of the resources on the CD-ROM.

• • •

The Evidence-Based Practice of
IPS Supported Employment

CHAPTER 1

Overview of IPS Supported Employment

IPS supported employment helps people with severe mental illness work at regular jobs of their choosing. Although variations of supported employment exist, in this book IPS (Individual Placement and Support) refers to the evidence-based practice of supported employment.

Characteristics of IPS Supported Employment

The practice of IPS supported employment described in this book includes the following characteristics:

1 It is an evidence-based practice.

2 IPS supported employment practitioners focus on client strengths.

3 Work can promote recovery and wellness.

4 Practitioners work in collaboration with state vocational rehabilitation.

5 It uses a multidisciplinary team approach.

6 Services are individualized and long-lasting.

7 The IPS approach changes the way mental health services are delivered.

Evidence-Based Practice

There are many types of vocational programs for people with disabilities, for example, sheltered workshops, work adjustment programs, supervised work crews, and community job programs. Further, each agency may have a different version of these services—a work adjustment program in one agency might be different from a work adjustment program someplace else. Often clients simply receive services based on ideas that program administrators assume will lead to successful outcomes. Yet we're learning that many of our hunches about how to help people with work have been false.

To counter this problem, researchers have studied vocational services (in regular agencies) to learn which approaches are most effective. The evidence-based practice of supported employment, IPS, uses the strategies that were found to result in the best outcomes. The research demonstrates that people are about three times more likely to work in regular part-time or full-time jobs when participating in IPS services rather than other vocational services. Over time, researchers will continue to focus on refining and improving the IPS supported employment model.

IPS Supported Employment Practitioners Focus on Client Strengths

IPS supported employment practitioners cover a broad range of positions. Employment specialists, vocational rehabilitation counselors, benefits specialists, psychiatrists, mental health workers (sometimes called *case managers*), nurses, residential workers, substance use counselors, and occupational therapists all play a role in supporting individuals' work efforts through this approach. Successful practitioners believe that their clients have strengths, talents, experiences, and abilities that can be used in the workplace. They know that even if their clients haven't been successful in the past, the right environment or right supports can make all the difference. IPS practitioners are creative and persistent problem solvers. They believe in client choice. Even when they don't fully understand the reasons for a client's preferences, they defend the person's right to have services based on his or her personal values. IPS practitioners are willing to take risks. They know that none of us has a guarantee of success at anything we try. However, experienced practitioners usually have many stories about people who were successful at goals that initially appeared to be impractical.

Work and Recovery

IPS is based on the idea (which is supported by research) that working in a regular job in everyday work environments, rather than sheltered employment, enhances people's lives, promotes wellness, and reduces stigma. Every person recovering from mental illness needs to define recovery in his or her own way. For some people, recovery could mean being a parent again. For others, it could mean managing symptoms enough to feel in control. However, for the great majority of people who are pursuing recovery, work is a central theme.

■ ■ ■

Work for . . . [people with] serious mental illnesses is much more than just a job. Jobs bring dignity, increased opportunities for self-determination. Jobs are people's identity. Jobs are where people meet their friends, and frequently their life partners. And a job is an opportunity to break the cycle of dependence and isolation that so often accompanies a severe mental illness, or any disability. A dozen years ago I was sitting at home, smoking cigarettes, drinking coffee and pacing the floor day after day. A job working evenings . . . broke that cycle. I got out of the house. I was able to have some income again. Most important, that job gave me back hope that there was a future.

—Doug DeVoe, testimony before the Ticket to Work Program
Evaluation Committee on March 8, 2001

IPS Partnership with State Vocational Rehabilitation

Each state, as well as the District of Columbia and U.S. territories, supports a division of Vocational Rehabilitation (VR) that has offices throughout the state to provide vocational rehabilitation services for individuals with disabilities. The focus of VR is to help people find gainful employment. Rehabilitation counselors at these offices sometimes provide direct services to clients and other times work with local programs (such as IPS programs) that provide side-by-side assistance to individuals who wish to work.

People who have access to both IPS and VR services have better outcomes than those who participate in only one service. We encourage IPS programs to share cases with VR and also to meet with rehabilitation counselors on a regular basis (at least once a month) to ensure seamless service delivery.

Eligibility for VR is determined on a person-by-person basis using three criteria established in federal law. To be eligible for VR services, a person must

1. Have a physical, mental, or sensory impairment that constitutes or results in a substantial impediment to employment

2. Be able to benefit from VR services in terms of an employment outcome, though it is presumed that clients can benefit unless assessments are unsuccessful

3. Require substantial VR services to prepare for, secure, retain, or regain employment

Rehabilitation counselors help clients develop an employment plan. When IPS and VR are working together, the rehabilitation counselor, employment specialist, and client all collaborate on a plan that is based on the job seeker's goals and preferences. VR may also be able to fund certain services in the plan, such as job development, job coaching, and follow-along services. In some cases, VR assists clients with job training, education programs, and purchase of work uniforms, tools, or other items necessary for work. Services received vary from person to person but must be related to the employment plan.

It's important that employment specialists and mental health practitioners understand that the VR system operates under different rules than the mental health system. For instance, rehabilitation counselors must show that the people on their caseloads are making steady progress toward their individual employment goals. Rehabilitation counselors also have higher caseloads than employment specialists; in fact, caseloads over 100 are not uncommon. Each counselor at VR is accountable for the number of people who are closed successfully each year. Take time to learn about the policies under which rehabilitation counselors operate and remember that the mental health system and VR share one very important goal: both want to help people with disabilities return to the workforce. To find your local VR office, visit your state office of Vocational Rehabilitation: http://askjan.org. Select "Job Seekers," then scroll down to "Federal, State, and Local Resources." Click on it and then scroll down to "Vocational Rehabilitation Agencies (VR)." For more information about VR, see chapter 10.

Multidisciplinary Program Structure
IPS is delivered by a team that includes the following people:

- the person who wants to work (sometimes called client, worker, or job seeker)
- an employment specialist
- a vocational rehabilitation (VR) counselor from the state
- a case manager or counselor
- a psychiatrist

- family members (with client permission)
- other staff members who are involved with the person

Although the employment specialist is the team member who usually spends the most time helping the client with jobs, other team members can also pitch in. For example, the psychiatrist might adjust medications so the person is less drowsy on the job, or a case manager might encourage the person to continue working on personal employment goals. All team members take on the responsibility of keeping their eyes open for businesses that might have the type of jobs the client would like. Finally, team members talk together often so that everyone is aware of current developments.

Individualized and Long-Lasting Supported Employment Services
In IPS, services are designed specifically for each person. In fact, no two people participating in the program should receive identical services. Employment specialists and clients work side by side (and with suggestions from the team) to determine which strategies will work best for the individual client.

Prevocational activities such as vocational tests, work samples, work readiness groups, and work adjustment activities are *not* part of IPS. Like most of us, clients don't want to jump through hoops before going back to work. Further, employment specialists don't want clients to feel as though they must prove their ability to work. Rather, employment specialists try to communicate a hopeful attitude about everyone's ability to work by starting the job search soon after the person expresses interest in work.

This means that instead of spending time on testing and work readiness activities, the employment specialist and client begin by gathering a variety of information, including historical information from the client, and (with permission) talking with family members and previous employers. The employment specialist studies the client's clinical record and consults with other members of the team. The client and employment specialist work together to create a plan designed to help the person obtain a job as quickly as possible. They recognize that the best assessment and training for getting a job is often getting a job; experience is the best teacher.

The vocational assessment is an ongoing process of trying out regular jobs in the community. Each job experience provides new information about the person as a worker. There are no failures in IPS supported employment—all jobs are viewed positively. No matter the outcome, each job teaches something about the

Duplicating this page is illegal. Do not copy this material without written permission from the publisher.

5

person as a worker and helps with planning for the next job. For example, one person who was fired from a job in a retail store after three days learned that he developed paranoid thoughts when he was around a lot of people. In his next job search, he looked for a quiet work setting.

Finally, IPS supported employment programs provide job supports for as long as the person wants help. At first the program has frequent (weekly or even daily) contact with the person starting a new job. Over time the amount of services might wax and wane. For instance, one person who had been working for six months met with his employment specialist once each month. The employment specialist looked at his earnings to reassure him that he was not going to lose benefits unexpectedly, asked how the job was going, and made a quick call to the employer. When the client's mother died, the man's symptoms increased, and the work situation began to deteriorate. During this period, the employment specialist met with the person several times each week and had weekly contact with the employer until the crisis passed. Eventually, the person's job stabilized, and he no longer felt that he needed support from the employment specialist. His case manager continued to ask about the job and helped him report his income.

IPS Supported Employment—A Change for Mental Health Services

The benefits of IPS become obvious to mental health workers as they observe people with severe mental illness going back to work. Psychiatrists and mental health workers who have assumed that many of their clients were not ready to work begin to see that some of those people do so successfully. They begin to appreciate that clients really do know when it is the right time to try work. Further, they observe that many people cast off the "mental patient" identity as they go back to work.

After IPS has been operating for a while, ripples of those changes move throughout the agency, reflecting a general shift in attitude among clients and providers alike. The expectation that people with severe mental illness can work—and should have the opportunity to work—becomes the norm rather than the exception. Services delivered by the agency begin to focus on what is important and meaningful to people with severe mental illness.

• • •

Principles of IPS Supported Employment

Before we discuss specific skills, it's important to recognize that IPS supported employment is based on a set of principles. The skills that you will learn are most effective when they build on the foundation of these principles.

The Seven Principles of IPS Supported Employment

These seven principles are well supported by research:

1. Zero exclusion

2. Integration of employment and mental health services

3. Competitive employment

4. Benefits planning

5. Rapid job search

6. Follow-along supports

7. Client preferences are honored

Zero Exclusion

All clients who want to participate in supported employment are eligible.

One of the research findings that surprised many people was that motivation to work was such a strong predictor of success. It seems natural to assume that people who use drugs or who have a lot of symptoms of mental illness would not be successful at work, but this is incorrect. *The truth is that we don't have a crystal ball when it comes to figuring out who is going to be successful at work.* Sometimes even people who are ambivalent about getting a job just need some support and encouragement so that they can build up their confidence about being able to work.

Example:

ENCOURAGEMENT CREATES OPPORTUNITIES

George was in his thirties, had recently been discharged from a long-term hospitalization, and still had delusions. George said that he was interested in going to work, but then refused to go to his first appointment with the VR counselor because he was having psychotic thoughts, including the belief that he was dead. Although the employment specialist was frustrated, the VR counselor talked to George about a new appointment, and the team worked together to help George develop an employment plan. George found a job with help from an employment specialist and worked at the same job for almost two years.

Practitioners need to be advocates for clients and educate others that people with mental illness have the right to work. When the IPS model is in place, case managers and employment specialists don't discourage people from working based on any of these factors:

- psychiatric diagnosis
- symptoms
- work history
- substance use
- cognitive impairment
- missed appointments
- grooming
- legal history
- cognitive problems

Integration of Employment and Mental Health Services

Frequent communication between team members is key.

Employment specialists who have been on the job for a while know how frustrating it is when the case manager encourages a client to drop out of the vocational process or when a psychiatrist changes someone's medications three days into a new job without informing the IPS team. Likewise, clients report that it is frustrating when they hear different messages from different service providers.

To avoid these problems, all of the people working with a client need to work as a team. Employment specialists, case managers, counselors, substance use specialists, psychiatrists, nurses, and others meet at least once a week to discuss strategies that will help clients meet their goals. For example, the team might try to determine how to help a person who is experiencing medication side effects on the job. Or they might collaborate on a plan to provide extra support to someone who is about to start a new job. Team members also touch base with each other between meetings for quick updates and problem-solving sessions. After talking together, the treatment team shares their ideas with the client, who makes the final decisions about services.

Many people participating in IPS programs have family members or others whom they would like to involve in their employment plan. We urge employment specialists to reach out to people identified by their clients. Throughout this manual we also stress the importance of obtaining the client's permission before contacting family members. Talk to your supervisor to make sure you understand your agency's policies for seeking permission to include others, such as family members, in the employment plan.

Finally, integration of services also refers to good service coordination with state Vocational Rehabilitation (VR). Some IPS programs integrate services with VR by inviting rehabilitation counselors to attend weekly IPS meetings. Others meet monthly at the VR office to review clients on shared caseloads. Still others reserve office space at their agency for rehabilitation counselors to use. More information about collaboration with VR is included in chapter 10.

Competitive Employment

IPS supported employment emphasizes competitive jobs at competitive wages.

Competitive jobs

- are part time or full time
- are regular jobs in the community (not jobs reserved for people with disabilities)
- pay at least minimum wage
- have the same pay and benefits as everyone else who holds those positions
- don't have time limits determined by the mental health or vocational agency

Competitive work is valued for several reasons. First, most clients express a strong preference for competitive work over sheltered work and a desire to work in community settings rather than segregated settings. Second, competitive work promotes the integration of individuals with psychiatric disabilities into the community. Third, almost all people report that they feel better about themselves as they see they are able to work in regular jobs, that their work is valued, and that they can contribute to society. Finally, experience shows that most people can successfully work at real-world jobs without prior participation in training programs, enclaves, or volunteer jobs.

Duplicating this page is illegal. Do not copy this material without written permission from the publisher.

9

EXAMPLES OF JOBS	COMPETITIVE OR NOT?
Working as a landscaper on a work crew with people who have disabilities. Earning a bit more than minimum wage.	Not a competitive job. This job is set aside for people with disabilities.
Working as a landscaper for a local golf course, April through September. Earning minimum wage.	Competitive job. Many people, with or without disabilities, work at seasonal jobs.
Working full time changing oil in a local garage.	Competitive job.
Working two hours each week in a bookstore earning minimum wage.	Competitive job.
Working at the mental health agency in a janitorial position. The agency encourages clients to apply for the job but also advertises locally. In spite of the advertisements, clients fill 90 percent of janitor positions.	Not a competitive job. This job is essentially set aside for clients of the mental health agency.
Working as a peer specialist at a mental health agency.	Assuming that the peer specialists are treated like other practitioners at the agency (that is, receive similar wages and have access to records), these jobs are competitive. Although the jobs are set aside, only someone with a mental illness is qualified to work as a peer specialist.
Working in a sheltered workshop that also hires people from the community who do not have disabilities. Having a vocational counselor at the workshop who writes a treatment plan to help the person improve work performance. Earning $1 above minimum wage.	Not a competitive job, because the workers without disabilities do not have treatment plans written with an employee of the workshop.
Babysitting for neighbors.	Not a competitive job, unless the person is recording and reporting income to the IPS and paying Social Security taxes.
Working in a nursing home in a food server position that was set up by an employment program. The position pays above minimum wage and is set up to last for six months.	Not a competitive job. This job is a transitional employment position with time limits imposed by the employment program.

> ▪ ▪ ▪
>
> *Working at a regular job—not a sheltered job—shows that people with mental illness are as good at work as anyone. It helps me feel equalized with other people. . . . My background is in acting and I like my job in the theater. Even though I'm part of the house staff, seeing those performers up on stage and hearing the applause is great!*
>
> —Jesse

Benefits Planning

People who receive entitlements need personalized planning when they are considering employment.

Fear of losing benefits, such as Social Security, Medicaid, or housing subsidies, is a major reason that clients sometimes avoid employment. In fact, it's wise to consider how work will affect finances and medical benefits, which is why IPS supported employment includes counseling clients about benefits and work incentives.

Benefits planning is also helpful to clients who are already working. Increases in hours or pay raises may affect benefit eligibility in ways that clients may not know or remember, particularly if they received the information long ago. Further, other changes (for example, the birth of a child or the loss of food stamps) can impact a person's financial situation. Therefore, benefits planning should be an ongoing service.

Benefits planning should only be provided by practitioners who have reliable, up-to-date information and who are willing to double-check the facts. Benefits planners should receive extensive training about work incentives and various sources of income. They need to be prepared to answer a wide range of questions, for example, questions about the effect of earned income on a dependent child, or the effects of a full-time job on VA (Veterans Affairs) benefits. Knowledge of work incentives such as PASS (Plan for Achieving Self-Support) Plans and earned Impairment-Related Work Expenses is also needed. The rules governing these programs change regularly, so ongoing training is critical. We do not advocate that employment specialists provide benefits planning to their clients unless they

Duplicating this page is illegal. Do not copy this material without written permission from the publisher.

11

have had extensive training in work incentives. Teams may wish to designate one person to help with benefits planning since learning about benefits is a time-intensive process.

Rapid Job Search

The process of looking for work begins soon after a client begins meeting with an employment specialist.

Rapid job search refers to a process of quickly initiating face-to-face contact with potential employers. Employment specialists help most clients explore job opportunities within one month of starting the IPS supported employment program. There are a number of reasons to jump right into the job search:

1. Beginning the search early demonstrates to clients that you are taking their goals seriously.

2. A quick job search also demonstrates your belief that clients have the necessary strengths and work skills for a job.

3. For some clients, there is a window of opportunity when it comes to going back to work. Exploring jobs in the community is one way to take advantage of that motivation—people start to get excited as they see the possibilities.

Some clients may have tried other vocational programs that required vocational testing, work adjustment, work readiness groups, or other prevocational activities. Many people find this process frustrating or demeaning and, as a result, drop out of the program. In contrast, many clients are interested in IPS because of the rapid job search.

To decide which type of jobs to apply for, the employment specialist and client spend a few weeks talking about the client's work history, employment goals, and other factors related to a job. The employment specialist records this information on a form usually referred to as the career profile. (In the past, this form was typically referred to as a *vocational profile* but because IPS programs also help with career development and supported education, we now use the term *career profile*.)

Developing a good working relationship is one of the main goals during these initial meetings. Therefore, specialists avoid firing question after question at the client. Employment specialists may ask if they can take a few notes, but they keep their focus on the person, ask good follow-up questions, and try to understand what is important to the client. The employment specialist does not attempt to complete the entire profile in one meeting. As the client begins the job search, and even after the person begins working, the employment specialist will add more information to the career profile.

After the employment specialist and client have become acquainted and have had a chance to talk about jobs, they begin developing a job search plan. (In many cases, the person will also have a state vocational rehabilitation counselor who joins them to develop the job search plan.) The plan should include enough details that anyone who reads it would start to get a picture of the client and the type of work the client wants. For example, the goal might read: "John will find a job that is about twenty hours per week and that will allow him to use his skills to help other people. John is interested in home health care, senior centers, and faith-based organizations." The plan would also include the specific steps that the client, employment specialist, and VR counselor will take to secure a job.

Follow-Along Supports

Individualized assistance to working clients is available as long as needed and desired.

As with the job search, planning the follow-along supports should be a thoughtful process. Because each person has specific needs for follow-along supports, each plan should be unique. Although employment specialists provide many of the follow-along supports needed, case managers, therapists, and others can also help.

Follow-along supports should include offers to help with career development. This is beneficial since some clients' preferences for types of jobs or job responsibilities may change after working for a while. Others will become interested in school or specialized training. IPS supported employment programs can help clients explore their options, apply for financial aid, find a tutor, and so on.

When there is a good job match and the job has been stable for a long time, the mental health practitioner (for example, case manager or therapist) may be selected to provide job supports. This move allows the employment specialist to take on new clients. When case managers provide job supports, the employment specialist continues to attend the weekly team meeting and occasionally ask mental health practitioners about the person's job. If the client begins to have problems at work, the employment specialist is ready to share expertise or reopen the person's case.

Clients who are working should not be transferred off the IPS team too quickly. The treatment team should consider all the current issues in the person's life and job before making this move. Further, the team should discuss the job supports that the person needs and consider whether the case manager can provide such supports. On average, clients will receive IPS services for a year after starting work.

Client Preferences Are Honored

Client preferences strongly influence the type of job that is sought, the nature of support provided by the employment specialist, and decisions about disclosing one's disability to the employer.

This principle trumps all of the others. IPS supported employment is about empowering people to have choices and options in their lives. Even the *way* that services are provided should be based on client preferences.

But providing services based on a person's preferences is harder than it sounds. Sometimes employment specialists unintentionally lead clients in one direction or another. Clients may try to please employment specialists and say what they think staff want to hear. This is like building a house on a bad foundation. Eventually, everyone's work will fall apart if it is not built upon the client's values, interests, and own way of doing things. The person has to be invested in the plan or it will not work. As a practitioner, you have to take responsibility for understanding and following the client's preferences.

Clients often say that they want to do the same type of work that they have done in the past. This may be because they really enjoyed that work, or because they don't believe an employer will hire them to do a different type of job. It's also true that some people just aren't aware of the variety of jobs available in their community. If a person who has done food prep in the past says that he wants another food prep job, for example, find out what it is about food prep that interests him. Talk to him about other jobs for which he is qualified. Some people find it easiest to learn about new jobs by seeing the workplace in action. Offer to take them out to visit job sites related to their interests.

When clients find jobs in their area of interest, they report that they like their jobs better and they stay at those jobs longer. Job preferences can be related to type of work, job location, hours of work each week, type of work environment, and so on. Try not to panic if someone has many preferences. It's natural to feel a little overwhelmed, but meeting client preferences from the beginning can prevent problems down the road.

Clients also have preferences about the way that they get help. For instance, one person may want help role-playing an interview, while another may wish for the employment specialist to sit in on job interviews. Another example relates to job coaching. Most people do *not* want someone to go on the job and help them learn their work, but some report that coaching is helpful.

Preferences about specific services are often related to whether the person wants to share information about his or her disability with an employer. This is sometimes referred to as *disclosure of a disability*. Some people think it is very helpful to have an employment specialist speak to potential employers on their behalf and work with their employers over time. For example, one client said that he wanted his employer to know about his panic attacks up front so that he wouldn't feel anxious about trying to hide a panic attack on the job. He was relieved to have an employment specialist explain to his boss that he might occasionally take an unscheduled break but that he would make up the time later. Other people are concerned about stigma regarding mental illness and possible job discrimination and, therefore, do not want the employment specialist to talk to employers. In those cases, the employment specialist provides ideas and support behind the scenes. The goal is to help the client feel comfortable and in control throughout the vocational process.

Example:

WORK PLANS BASED ON THE NEEDS AND INTERESTS OF THE PERSON

Cheryl was working with a man in his fifties who had not been employed for the past five years. He lived in an assisted living apartment where he was able to have a dog. The problem was that every time he left the apartment, his dog started barking and the neighbors complained. The man was afraid that if he went to work, the dog would bark a lot, and he would be forced to get rid of the dog. The employment specialist's willingness to take his problem seriously made all the difference.

Cheryl talked to the other members of her IPS team, as well as the client's case manager. They tried to brainstorm possible jobs that might allow the client to bring his dog to work and then ultimately suggested hiring a pet sitter for the man's dog. The client liked the idea of a pet sitter and was able to work out an arrangement with someone he knew.

In this example, the team's first response was to try to come up with a job that would allow dogs. This demonstrates a willingness to be creative and flexible. It's

Duplicating this page is illegal. Do not copy this material without written permission from the publisher.

15

okay that their first idea didn't work out. What's important is that they were willing to look for something rare, rather than tell the client that he was being unreasonable. It was also impressive that they thought of more than one solution to meet the person's preferences.

CONCLUSION

IPS supported employment principles are directly related to client outcomes. Programs that follow the guidelines of the evidence-based practice help a greater number of people find employment. For example, a twelve-state project demonstrated that, on average, programs could maintain 40–50 percent employment at any given time. High-performing programs (those with outcomes in the top quarter) were able to achieve outcomes of 50 percent employment or higher on a quarterly basis. However, IPS principles are not a replacement for creativity, skills, and knowledge. Employment specialists, VR counselors, and supervisors must be knowledgeable about the local job market and the needs of employers. They must have skills for interacting with clients, employers, and mental health workers. And creativity is critical in order to help clients discover good job matches, job accommodations, and individualized supports. IPS supported employment challenges practitioners to be extremely thoughtful in their approach.

• • •

TOOLS TO LEARN MORE ABOUT IPS SUPPORTED EMPLOYMENT PRINCIPLES:

- You can watch some short videos about IPS supported employment by going to www.dartmouth.edu/~ips. Select "Resources," then "Videos." Select "Introducing IPS Supported Employment."

  From that list of videos, we suggest *3 Faces, 3 Lives* (available with English or Spanish subtitles) or *Introduction* (available with Spanish subtitles) to hear first-person accounts of working and recovering from mental illness.

- Ask the Dartmouth IPS Supported Employment Team questions about this approach by going to www.dartmouth.edu/~ips. Select "ASK about IPS." Submit your question and the team will post an answer online within a couple of weeks.

- Consider taking an online course about IPS supported employment. Go to www.dartmouth.edu/~ips. Select "Online Training in IPS SE."

Skills for Employment Specialists and IPS Supported Employment Supervisors

Developing Skills for Interviewing Clients

Interacting with clients is a central task of IPS supported employment. Let's start with a few basics. Effective practitioners believe the following:

- It is important to know each person as an individual.
- Clients benefit from relationships with people who are hopeful.
- Every person deserves to be treated with respect.
- Most people struggle when they try to make a big change in their lives, whether or not they have a mental illness.

People with mental illnesses are people first. In order to help people, you'll need to get to know each person as an individual. Think of someone who is on your caseload now. What do you know about that person's values? Who are the important people in his life? How does she spend her time? How would he like his life to be different? Knowing all of this won't just help you think of good job ideas, it will also help you figure out how to provide support in ways that work for that person. (See an example of an individualized approach on page 20.)

You may sometimes hear others talk about clients in a disrespectful manner. They may believe that the way they talk behind the scenes doesn't affect the work they do, but they're wrong. People who are effective practitioners speak about clients in hopeful and respectful ways. They believe that clients have the right to make their own choices about how to live. They do not feel resentful when clients make choices that don't result in successful outcomes. Rather, successful practitioners believe that people learn from their mistakes and make progressively better choices over time. They take things in stride knowing that individuals can only change at their own pace—not on someone else's schedule.

Think of the last time that you tried to make a big change in your life (for example, losing weight, being patient with your children, or giving up cigarettes). Did you find that you had more motivation on some days than others? Did you fail to follow through on some of your goals? Everyone can think of some missed opportunities in their lives, but it's rarely helpful to have someone preach to us about the ways that we should do better. We're more likely to benefit from knowing that someone believes in us.

Likewise, you may find that some clients have trouble following through with

Example:

AN INDIVIDUALIZED APPROACH

An IPS supported employment team was discussing a client who had recently found a job. They were trying to decide which follow-along supports would be most helpful. A few team members commented that this individual didn't have any personal supports. However, one employment specialist spoke up to say that the person was close with an aunt who lived out of state. The client wrote to the aunt on a regular basis, and they talked on the phone when they could afford the calls. The employment specialist knew this because she had visited the client at home. The team decided it would be a good idea to ask the client if she would like to invite her aunt to a conference call to talk about the employment plan.

everything on their employment plan. Going back to work is a big change. Try to think of ways to help people while being respectful of who they are and how they want to approach employment. Remember, people are more likely to make positive changes if they feel that you value their strengths and see them as capable individuals.

Three Steps to Successful Interactions

In your interactions with the people on your caseload, several specific steps are critical:

1. Developing a good working relationship
2. Using effective interviewing skills
3. Incorporating interview skills into your daily work

This section describes the skills you will need for each of these steps.

Developing a Relationship with Each Client

The first step is helping the person feel comfortable with you. Clients are probably wondering what it will be like to work with you. They may have attended other social service programs in the past, and it is doubtful that all of those experiences were positive. Some practitioners talk down to clients, ignore things that clients feel are important, and even blame clients instead of helping. Your job now is to earn the person's trust.

First impressions are important. Introduce yourself and describe your role in a friendly way. For example, "Hi, I'm Juanita Arnett, and I am an employment specialist. I work closely with Emily and she told me you're thinking about going back to work. I'm interested in talking to you about work and how I can help." The tone is straightforward, down to earth, and earnest. Use your own words, but try to convey from the beginning that you want to help the client reach his or her goals, but he or she is the one who is in charge of setting those goals.

Next, ask the person to tell you about his or her hopes for a job. For example, say, "Please tell me your thoughts about a job." Here the key is to be a good listener. Try to get the person to do most of the talking. One way to do that is to ask open-ended questions—the kind that can't really be answered with a "yes" or "no." For example, instead of asking, "Do you want to get another job in construction?" you could ask, "What kind of job are you thinking about?"

Another technique to help a person open up is to *reflect* back what the person has said. This technique is called *reflective listening*. For example, after the person has talked for several minutes and has come to a stop, summarize what you have heard. For example, "If I understand you correctly, you have been unemployed for several years and you are worried about working too much because you are out of practice. So you want to start with just a few hours per week. Does that sound right?" Reflection lets clients know that you are listening and trying to understand their point of view. It also provides an opportunity for people to correct any misunderstandings and to share additional information. For more on reflective listening, see page 23.

At the end of a series of open-ended questions, summarize what you think you have heard to ensure that you understand what is important to the person. For example, "You have experience fixing small machines and doing light construction around your family's farm. You'd like to find an indoor job where you could use some of those skills. Does that sound right?"

As you develop a relationship, remember that if you are an employment specialist, you should not attempt to provide services for which the case manager or therapist is responsible. Employment specialists often wonder what to do when symptoms of mental illness arise, for example, if the person says something that does not make sense or asks about how to handle symptoms of mental illness, such as "What if I have a panic attack on the job?" "I lost my last job because I started preaching to the customers—I guess I was getting manic." It's helpful to acknowledge that these may be important areas of concern but not ones on which you are an expert. This is why you work as part of a team, and the client needs to understand the different roles of the team members.

You might say, for example, "Sounds like it's stressful to have voices. I think it would be a good idea to invite your case manager and psychiatrist to join us in this discussion since they know more about these symptoms than I do. Maybe we

GOOD INTERVIEWING INVOLVES THE FOLLOWING:

➤ demonstrating active listening with reflective listening

➤ asking open-ended questions

➤ expressing empathy

➤ maintaining focus

➤ avoiding advice

➤ staying positive

➤ reframing events

➤ emphasizing strengths

➤ avoiding arguments

➤ handling personal disclosure

➤ closing the interview

can all come up with a plan together to help you manage those symptoms when you're at work." Team meetings are a great place to brainstorm coping mechanisms or job accommodations that will help the person feel more comfortable on the job. However, don't wait for the next treatment team meeting to relay *new* information about symptoms to the rest of the team. Communicating information in a timely manner allows the appropriate team member to quickly offer options, such as a medication change or other intervention if the person's symptoms worsen.

As mentioned above, some people have developed coping mechanisms to deal with symptoms. Being aware of this information can help you better plan a job. For example, some people know that they are likely to hear voices when they are alone, and others know they'll hear voices when they are in a crowd. Some people might even have strategies to control the voices, such as focusing on a task or starting a conversation. In other words, to the extent that symptoms are relevant to employment, you need to try to understand them. To the extent that symptoms are relevant to treatment, you need to let other members of the team address them. If you're not sure about a particular situation, talk it over with the team.

Good interviewing skills are the bedrock of building a working relationship. In the following section, we discuss several aspects of good interviewing.

Effective Interviewing Skills

Good interviewing involves the following:

- demonstrating active listening with reflective listening
- asking open-ended questions

- expressing empathy
- maintaining focus
- avoiding advice
- staying positive
- reframing events
- emphasizing strengths
- avoiding arguments
- handling personal disclosure
- closing the interview

Examples in this section often demonstrate the use of more than one technique, as clients are often best served when techniques are combined. For this reason, you may wish to read this section several times.

DEMONSTRATING ACTIVE LISTENING WITH REFLECTIVE LISTENING

An employment specialist needs to be a good listener. People with mental illness often complain that professionals do not listen to them. It's important to fully understand what the person is saying before offering information, suggestions, or ideas. One feature of active listening is reflecting back to the person what you think you've heard. This lets the person know that you've been listening carefully and that you are interested in his or her views.

Example:

Jean:

I don't want to lose my benefits. I knew someone who went to work and then Social Security cut her off. I've been on Social Security for years, and I'm not saying that I don't want to work, but I don't want to work if I'm going to lose my benefits.

Eli:

You definitely want to keep your benefits. (Reflection)

Reflective listening allows clients to hear what they have said, and it gives them an opportunity to explain more about what they mean.

Example:

Jean:

My boss just walked into the office and starting yelling at me for dropping the call when I transferred it. He has no idea how many things I am trying to do at once. Furthermore, there were other people standing right there. He's such a jerk.

Eli:

You were angry when he commented on your work. (Reflection)

Jean:

That's right. I don't mind him telling me how I can do my job better, but I didn't like him doing it in front of my co-workers. I don't need that.

In this example, the employment specialist used reflective listening by paraphrasing what he heard the client say. Jean then explained that she was more upset about being corrected in front of other workers than about the criticism itself.

Example:

Tracy:

I go to my mom's most days for a little while in the afternoon. Sometimes I stay for dinner.

Rachel:

Sounds like you are close to your mom. Should we meet with her to talk about your employment plan? She might have some good ideas for jobs since she knows you so well.

Tracy:

I'm not sure. What would we talk about?

Rachel:

We could talk about the jobs that you have had in the past, ideas for new jobs. . . . What concerns do you have about a meeting with your mom? (Open-ended question)

Tracy:

I think it would be okay to talk about jobs, but I don't want to talk about my drinking. It just gets her upset, and I hate it when she starts nagging me about drinking. I'm an adult.

Rachel:

So, you think it would be okay to meet with your mom as long as we don't discuss anything related to drinking. (Reflection)

Tracy:

That's right.

Example:

Cheryl:

I really need to make some money, but I can only work while my kids are in school. I wouldn't mind working full time, but I don't want to put them in day care. My mom used to babysit for me, but she's having back problems, so that's not an option right now.

Harlan:

You want a job with hours during the school day. (Reflection)

Example:

Lenny:

I've never worked with animals before, but I've always had dogs, and spending time with my dogs is the best.

Asunción:

How do you spend time with your dogs? (Open-ended question)

Lenny:

Play with them, take them to the park. . . . I was thinking about grooming dogs because I groom my own dogs. I also saw a movie where someone walked dogs for money. I think those jobs would be all right, though I'm not sure if I could get hired because I don't have experience.

Asunción:

What other jobs working with animals have you thought about? (Open-ended question)

Lenny:

I definitely don't want to work in a shelter—too depressing. I guess if I couldn't find anything else I could work in a pet store, but I don't want to just clean cages. I really want to work with the animals.

Asunción:

So, your ideal job is working directly with animals, for instance, grooming or walking dogs. (Reflection)

Lenny:

Right.

Reflective listening can also help interviewers discover that they have misunderstood the person being interviewed. If the person corrects your understanding, summarize again to make sure you have it right.

Example of a summary and correction:

Angie:

I've worked as a maid in a hotel, and I really hated that job. We only had twenty-two minutes to clean a room, and some of those rooms were a mess! In the summer it was really miserable because the air-conditioning wasn't on in all of the rooms. I also had a job where I cleaned a Laundromat at night after it closed down. The hours were terrible. I only got two hours a night, so it wasn't very much money, and I had to work from 11 p.m. to 1 a.m. I didn't feel safe going back and forth to work.

Tyrone:

So, you wouldn't want another cleaning job. (Reflection)

Angie:

I didn't say that. I didn't like the hours at the Laundromat job, but the work was okay. I worked alone and I could work at my own pace.

Tyrone:

Oh! And being made to work too fast at the hotel bothered you. Sounds like it is important to you to be able to work at your own pace. (Corrected reflection)

Angie:

Right.

Tyrone:

And you also want to feel safe coming and going to work. (Reflection)

Angie:

Definitely.

ASKING OPEN-ENDED QUESTIONS

Questions that can be answered with a "yes" or "no" provide only a little information. To get a conversation going, try open-ended questions that encourage a person to share more. For example, instead of asking, "Did you like working as a hairstylist?" an employment specialist could try, "I'm interested in your job at the salon. What did you like about the job?" It often helps to ask for additional information, such as "Would you tell me a little more about that?" and "Help me understand how the customers were picky." Open-ended questions are valuable not only because they bring forth more information, but also because the way that the person answers demonstrates whether the person understood the question. After a person begins to express employment preferences, ask open-ended questions to gain a deeper understanding of the person's interests. For example, "Please tell me more about your interest in animals." Don't rush to a conclusion or ask a closed-ended question. "Would you like to work in a factory?" or "Do you like working alone?" would be too narrow at this point. Keep asking open-ended questions:

- "What do you think you might like to do in the clothing industry?"
- "What do you know about nursing home jobs?"
- "When did you first become interested in landscaping and nursery work?"
- "Tell me about the jobs that you have had in the past."
- "What did you like about that job? What did you dislike?"
- "What is it about working as a hairstylist that interests you?"
- "Sounds like you're good at finding jobs—what's the secret to your success?"
- "Why did you decide to leave that job?"
- "What would people who know you say are your good qualities and strengths?"
- "How did you find that job?"

CLOSED-ENDED QUESTIONS	OPEN-ENDED QUESTIONS
Do you know how your benefits will be affected by a return to work?	Tell me how your benefits will be affected by a return to work.
Did you like that job?	What did you like about that job?
Did you find that job on your own?	How did you find that job?
Do you want me to talk to employers on your behalf?	What would be some of the possible advantages to having me talk to employers on your behalf? The possible disadvantages?
What was the felony for?	Tell me about the situation that led to that felony conviction.

Remember, closed-ended questions can be answered with one word, while open-ended questions elicit more conversation.

EXPRESSING EMPATHY

An empathic statement includes feeling words that describe the emotion that the person is experiencing.

Example:

Alison:

I can't believe I got fired. I checked the schedule and I wasn't supposed to work on Wednesday. How was I supposed to know that the schedule changed?

Hakim:

You feel angry that you were fired. (Expression of empathy)

Example:

Sharon:

I know that wasn't the right job for me. I've been through tough times before and I know that I'll come out of this better than ever. God will help me move forward. You have to learn from your experiences, and that's what I'm doing!

Rob:

You continue to feel hopeful. (Expression of empathy)

MAINTAINING FOCUS

Each appointment with an employment specialist should help clients with their employment goals. Although the specialist may occasionally let the conversation drift in order to learn more about clients' interests or how they spend their day, the specialist does this in a careful manner. Some casual conversation can help build a relationship or lead to new discoveries, but it shouldn't be the main focus of an appointment.

AVOIDING ADVICE

When clients say that professionals are not good listeners, they often mean that many professionals offer advice before really understanding the problem from the person's point of view. Giving advice is dangerous for several reasons:

1. It tends to shift the focus from clients coming up with their own solutions to relying on the professional to be the expert. Advice can foster dependency.

2. Some people feel like they should agree with their employment specialist in order to be cooperative and to please the specialist. That doesn't mean the person will follow through with the advice later.

3. Giving too much advice can be annoying. It's a reason that some people may tune out of the conversation.

Rather than giving advice, encourage clients to find their own solutions. One way to do that is to help identify different options and the advantages and disadvantages for each option. For example, an employment specialist might say, "So there are some days that you wake up feeling depressed, and on those days it's really hard to get out of bed and go to work. What are some different ways you could deal with that situation? What has worked for you in the past?" After the person has thought of some different strategies, the specialist could suggest, "Let's think about the positives and negatives of the different approaches." This strategy, as opposed to *telling* the person what to do, empowers the client to think and feel in control of the situation.

It also helps to talk to clients about what has worked for them in the past. Sometimes people are shy about bringing up their past successes but will talk about them if asked. Asking about past successes also reinforces that the employment specialist doesn't have all of the answers and that the client already has skills and experiences that are useful. For example, when developing a job search plan, the employment specialist may discover that the client has been able to find jobs on his or her own in the past. The client's job-seeking approaches may be a little different from what the specialist is used to, but they may be a good fit for the client's personal style.

In some instances, the employment specialist may honestly disagree with a client's plan. In this situation, the employment specialist could ask if it would be okay to share some strategies that have worked for other people. Because the employment specialist asks first, the client is much more likely to consider the ideas. However, if the client clearly wants to go with a plan that the employment specialist feels is not practical, the employment specialist needs to be honest *and* continue to support the person. For example, if someone absolutely does not want to give a two-week notice when quitting a job, the employment specialist can explain why he or she doesn't think that is an effective way to leave a job, but should also offer to help the person with a new job.

Example of effective interaction with client:

Peter:
I'm not going back to that job. I hate cleaning out the grease pit, and those other guys are jerks.

Calvin:
Well, you gave that job a try. It's been four weeks and you still don't like it. Have you already given notice?

Peter:
No, I'm not going back at all. It's a crummy job and I really don't care.

Calvin:

So it sounds like one of the advantages to walking off is that you don't have to go back to a job that you don't like. What are some other advantages to walking off? (Open-ended question)

Peter:

I can't think of any, but I don't want to go back, so that's important.

Calvin:

Okay. You don't want to go back and that's important. (Reflection) *On the other hand, there could be some advantages in giving notice. Your boss liked your work, and if we talk to him, I bet he will give you a good reference. What are some other possible advantages to giving notice?* (Avoiding advice; open-ended question)

Peter:

I don't care. When I walked out of work today, that was the last time. All I want to do now is get another job.

Calvin:

Okay. You really just want to focus on a new job. That's your choice. (Reflection) *I need to go talk to your boss since I have a relationship with him. Basically, I am going to thank him for working with our program and ask him to consider working with us in the future. But you and I can start looking for another job right away. I guess the key is to think about a job you might like better. . . .*

The only exception to letting the person lead is when someone's safety is at risk. In this situation, employment specialists let the client know what they are required by law to do and take the necessary actions to keep people safe. Talk to your supervisor to ensure that you understand your agency's policies for handling situations when safety is a concern.

STAYING POSITIVE

You may work with people who have a lot of challenges in their lives. Sometimes, you may feel overwhelmed just hearing about those challenges. It can help to talk to a supervisor or co-worker who is positive and can help you remember that people on your caseload have actually accomplished a lot.

It may also help to know that the great majority of people with mental illness are able to manage the symptoms of their illness, find meaningful activities and relationships, and move on with their lives. It's exciting to remember that for many people, going back to work is a central step in this process. The work that you do as an employment specialist is vital.

You can convey optimism to your clients by reminding them of tasks that they have done well, encouraging them to keep trying, and telling them that all people have discouraging experiences and failures whether they have a mental illness or not. If someone is really feeling discouraged, it can also be helpful for the person to have an opportunity to talk to someone else who has overcome similar barriers. Some agencies ask working clients if they would be willing to share their back-to-work stories through newsletters, public speaking, or meeting with a client and employment specialist for a chat about work. If you're interested in working out something like this at your agency, speak to your supervisor to ensure that you understand and follow policies on confidentiality and other related matters.

REFRAMING EVENTS

You can show optimism by reframing events in a more positive way. A client might feel depressed and become pessimistic after losing a job, for example, but the employment specialist can help the client think about the parts of that experience that were positive (that's the "re-frame").

Example of reframing:

Dan:

I just couldn't do the job. Everything moved too fast. They expected too much of me. How come everyone else could do it?

Jody:

It sounds like you are discouraged, but you worked there for two weeks. That's longer than you've worked for years, so it's a first bit of success. And I bet you learned some important things. (Reframing) *What kind of job do you think would be a better fit?*

Example of reframing:

Harlan:

You look like you're feeling a little down about not getting hired.

Ethel:

I could tell he liked me! He liked that I had experience taking care of my grandmother when she was sick, and I could tell that we clicked, but he just shut down when he heard about my history. I guess if I were a boss, I wouldn't hire someone with felonies, either.

Harlan:

The way that you interviewed in there was great—I could tell that you were building a relationship with the employer. And you've improved in the way that you talk about your criminal record, so that's another bit of success. You may not have gotten the job, but it was great practice. (Reframing) *I really believe that you will find a job.*

Ethel:

I guess so.

Harlan:

You know, many people in our program have found work in spite of felonies. It's a pretty common problem, to tell you the truth. Do you think it would help to talk to someone who found a good job in spite of a record? We could ask questions about how that person found a job.

Ethel:

Maybe. Do you know someone who has more than one felony, like me?

EMPHASIZING STRENGTHS

Much of a person's experience in the mental health system involves working on deficits. Symptoms, weaknesses, and problems are the targets of many treatments. Unfortunately, the constant emphasis on negative aspects of one's life can reinforce low self-esteem and beliefs that one is ineffective and doomed to fail.

Yet there are other ways to approach mental health treatment; the most common approach is called the *strengths model*. Emphasizing strengths means that you are always looking for strengths rather than weaknesses. Everyone has strengths, and strengths are the secret to any kind of success.

Some people are good with details, some are good with people, some with computers, and so on. They may also have weaknesses, but they generally succeed in work because they have found niches that allow them to use their strengths and avoid their weaknesses. In some cases, people are successful by working on a team—people on a team can fill in for each other's weaknesses. Employment specialists can help employers think about ways that work can be assigned to allow individuals to focus on duties that draw on their natural abilities. This is why it helps to ask about successes and strengths.

While interviewing people, as employment specialists, we want to uncover and understand clients' strengths. Do this by asking open-ended questions about the person's preferences, abilities, and experiences. For example, "What is your dream job and why?" "What kinds of work do you like?" "What kinds of tasks are you good at?" "What kind of setting do you feel comfortable in?" "Tell me about your best job experience." Another great question to use is "What else?" After someone has described a situation and then stops talking, try asking, "What else?" to be sure you fully understand the person's opinions.

Example of emphasizing client strengths:

Ruby:

So, you really liked working as a pharmacy tech. Why was that?

Shirley:

I liked working at a job that felt responsible. I knew that I had to be very careful to do the right things. And it felt like a professional job. It wasn't an entry-level job. I had to be certified to work in a pharmacy.

Ruby:

What else?

Shirley:

Well, I guess I liked helping the customers. I tried to be friendly and answered their questions about cheaper generics, things like that. I like working with people.

The person's preferences, abilities, and experiences are only some of the areas in which you can find strengths. Other areas could include the following:

- A person's support system. For example, some clients have family or friends who help encourage work and are available for practical help.
- The person's values. For example, honesty or a belief in "a full day's work for a full day's wages" can be assets.

- Resources. Some clients may have their own resources for transportation to work or may have friends and family who can provide job leads.

- Personality traits such as being friendly, being polite, or having a good sense of humor.

- A strong desire to work or to spend time in a particular environment.

AVOIDING ARGUMENTS

It's rarely helpful to confront or argue. Motivational interviewing teaches us that people are usually ambivalent about changing their behavior. That is, when considering a change, most people are able to see reasons *to change* as well as reasons *not to change*.

If an employment specialist pushes for change, clients will likely feel the need to defend their reasons not to change. Therefore, rather than challenging a belief that you disagree with, it is better to "roll with the resistance." For example, if a client says he does not want to go for an interview, you could explore the reasons why he does not or move on to another task. It would not be helpful to argue by pointing out that the job will be lost and insist he really must go for the interview.

Example of avoiding an argument:

Keith:

I don't want to tell employers about my felony. If they find out after I am hired, I'll just get fired. Whatever.

Carol:

How has that worked for you in the past—to avoid talking about the felony? (Open-ended question)

Keith:

It worked once. Sometimes it doesn't. But I don't think an employer will hire me if they know that I have a sex offense. Anyhow, it's none of their business.

Carol:

It's true that some employers won't hire based on that. However, I have been able to help people find jobs in spite of felonies. In fact, one of my clients who has a felony is working as an assembler. But it's your choice.

Keith:

Well, I think employers would look down on me if they knew.

Carol:

That would feel uncomfortable. (Empathetic reflection)

Keith:

I don't want to put it on my application.

Carol:

Okay. Then it sounds like the plan for now is that you won't talk about the felony and you'll take your chances. I need to be up front and let you know that I can't lie to employers. So, I won't be able to connect directly with employers on your behalf, but I'll help you with job leads, filling out applications, interviewing skills. . . . (Rolling with resistance to avoid an argument)

Keith:

That sounds good.

Carol:

Then let's try it for a while. If you ever want to revise the plan, we can talk about it again.

HANDLING PERSONAL DISCLOSURE

An issue that often comes up involves self-disclosure. In other words, some employment specialists wonder how much of their own personal information they should share with clients.

We recommend that employment specialists be friendly and share some casual information, while remembering their role is to be an employment specialist, not a friend. Almost all of the conversation should be about the client. However, if a client asks a question such as, "Where did you get those shoes?" you could easily answer. If a client asks a more personal question, you should be direct and explain that you're not comfortable answering the question. For example, if a client asks, "Are you Christian?" you might say, "I'm sorry, but I don't feel comfortable talking about that aspect of my life."

As a professional, you need to be honest and friendly in order to develop a relationship, but you also need to be clear that the task is to help the person with employment. Spending time with stories about your life or your problems is inappropriate and often exploitative.

Wrapping up an interview involves summarizing the meeting's progress and identifying the next steps. Both the meeting summary and the next steps are stated positively and focus on the client's goals.

Example of closing an interview:

George:

So, we managed to submit two online applications today. I've already been to the hardware store, and I know that the manager will set up an interview with anyone who calls him seventy-two hours after submitting an online application. That would be Thursday. Do you want to call him?

Sue:

Sure. I can do that. So, I can mention my experience and ask to meet the guy, right?

George:

That's right. Do you want to try it on me now?

Sue:

Hi. My name is Sue and I applied online on Monday. I wanted to let you know that I have experience working in a hardware store and I also used to have a job in light construction. Would it be possible to meet with you to talk about my experience?

George:

Perfect. So, you'll call the hardware store on Thursday, and I will go in person to the building supply store to try to talk to a manager. If the hardware manager schedules an interview with you, give me a call. Otherwise, we'll meet again next Monday at 1:00. Does that sound like a plan?

Sue:

Sounds good.

Incorporating Interview Skills into Your Daily Work

The techniques described in this section may sound fairly simple. However, as you incorporate these techniques into your regular work, you may find that it is difficult to remember all of the tips in this section. Becoming skilled in these methods will take time, but here are some activities that will help you along:

- Reread this section from time to time.

- Ask your supervisor to observe some of your interactions with clients and provide feedback about times that you could have used a technique described above.

- Ask to practice with a co-worker. One of you can play the employment specialist while the other plays the client, and then switch.

- Take advantage of any opportunities to attend trainings on motivational interviewing. Many of the techniques described here are included in basic motivational interviewing training. (You can also look for written material by Miller and Rollnick on the Internet and in bookstores.)

If you are a supervisor, please be sure to read the chapter written specifically for supervisors to learn more about helping practitioners improve their interactions with clients.

• • •

CHAPTER 4

Creating an Individualized Job Search Plan

In this chapter, we'll discuss the importance of gathering information for a good job match, providing information to clients about benefits, talking about disclosure, developing an employment plan, and engaging in a rapid job search (avoiding vocational testing and other preemployment activities).

IPS supported employment focuses on helping people find work that is specific to their preferences and needs. Employment specialists do not rely on jobs that are easily available, but instead try to help each person think about his or her past work experiences, skills, preferred work schedule, job location, and so on. All of this information is considered when developing the employment plan.

For all of us, job satisfaction is strongly related to the match between who we are and the characteristics of the job. One person is happy studying old manuscripts in the basement of a library; another thoroughly enjoys selling cars; and a third loves cooking in a busy kitchen. They all have good job matches and would not be comfortable in each other's positions. So it is with people who have a mental illness. A person who likes to be alone and out of doors is likely to prefer working as a groundskeeper at a golf course rather than as a salesperson in a busy store. This idea of job match is pretty simple, but the actual practice of helping people locate good job matches can be complex and creative.

How do you help someone make a good job match? It helps to gather as much information as possible about a person's interests, skills, past experiences,

coping strategies, symptoms, and treatment. Also, think about who the person is—where the person likes to go, how the person spends the day, his or her values, and so on.

Much of this comes from talking with the client. In the previous chapter, you learned that open-ended questions about past experiences, interests, daily activities, preferences for work settings, and so on, serve to develop an information base. The employment specialist can best learn some of this information while visiting job sites with the client and discussing the client's impressions. The employment specialist also reads the client's medical record, meets with the mental health treatment team, and, with the client's consent, may interview previous employers and family or friends.

For example, an IPS team in Illinois met to brainstorm good job matches for a person who was interested in the environment, books, and liberal politics. She didn't have a high school diploma, and she also had one felony related to drugs. On the other hand, this person had an engaging personality. The team came up with ideas such as working in a coffee house, a secondhand bookstore, and a small, progressive newspaper. The thought was that the person might be interested in the people she would meet in those jobs and might also feel like she would fit in.

Traditional approaches to assessment and evaluation, such as standardized pencil-and-paper tests, vocational evaluations, and work adjustment activities, are not adequate sources of information. They do not predict well, waste time, and discourage people who are ready to work.

Planning a job can often be done quickly, typically in a few meetings with some work between meetings. The important tasks are to collect information rapidly, consider it along with the client, and put it together in a plan. The job plan doesn't have to be perfect. A lot of employment plans change over time as clients experiment and learn more about what fits for them. People with mental illness often become ill early in life, before they finish education and establish a working life and career. Therefore, they often learn about work by trying different jobs. With each experience, the job plan can be updated and refined.

Julie Temple is an employment specialist who recognizes the benefits of looking for the right job match. She points out that it isn't possible to learn enough information about a person in one meeting. Julie explains how she uses several meetings to get to know her clients and then continues to help them refine their job goals even after the job search is under way.

■ ■ ■

An individualized employment goal isn't always something you can figure out overnight. To me, it includes looking at the person's strengths, but sometimes you have to work with someone for a while to figure out who the person really is. For instance, reviewing a person's past jobs is helpful, but the person might have other interests, as well. If someone says they want to do the same type of work that they've always done, I ask the person if they've ever thought of other kinds of jobs or if they know people who work in different types of jobs. I might look through the job openings with people and start discussions about different types of jobs or even go out with people and point out different kinds of jobs.

When a client and I come up with a job goal that is pretty specific, for instance, very limited number of work hours or very specific kinds of duties, I know that I may need to talk to employers about carving out a job or creating a specific position. So, that's when I need to get out there and talk to employers to find out about their businesses. While I'm doing that, I can get a feel for their willingness to develop a position that fits the person I am working with. Sometimes the employers that I've worked with in the past are helpful because we already have a relationship. Also, smaller employers seem to have an easier time making adjustments to positions. But you never know. I just had a very positive contact with a national company today.

Steps to Finding a Good Job Match

Working through a series of steps will help you understand your clients better and improve your chance of finding a good job match. These steps include

1. creating a career profile

2. gathering information from multiple sources

3. meeting outside the office

4. connecting clients to a benefits planner

5. discussing self-disclosure

6. including family members

7. maintaining engagement

8. conducting a work-based assessment

9. creating an employment plan

Creating a Career Profile

Assessment is a collaborative activity consisting of conversations with the client, mental health practitioners, family members (with permission), VR counselors, and others. The aim is to get to know the client, understand his or her goals, obtain a detailed work history (to understand what type of jobs and job supports might work best), and other information that will help the person succeed. Some people refer to this as an assessment or a career profile. (In the past, we used the term *vocational profile,* but because IPS programs also help with career development and supported education, we now use the term *career profile* more frequently.) The CD-ROM includes a sample career profile used by many programs, as well as a career profile face sheet. The career profile is typically based on a number of elements, including the following:

Work Goal

- ☐ person's short-term work goal in his or her own words
- ☐ person's preferences for type of work, setting, hours, wages, and disclosure of disability
- ☐ person's career goal

Work Background

- ☐ licenses and certifications
- ☐ military history
- ☐ previous jobs (titles, duties, dates, hours per week)
- ☐ reasons for leaving jobs
- ☐ positive experiences
- ☐ problems on jobs

Education History

- ☐ highest level of education obtained
- ☐ education and job training institutions attended

- ☐ degrees and certificates earned
- ☐ positive experiences with each education experience
- ☐ problems with each education experience
- ☐ goals for education or training

Work Skills

- ☐ job-seeking skills
- ☐ specific vocational skills
- ☐ aptitude
- ☐ interests (vocational and nonvocational)
- ☐ work habits relating to attendance, dependability, stress tolerance
- ☐ cognitive abilities or problems

Other Work-Related Factors

- ☐ transportation
- ☐ support from family and friends
- ☐ current living situation (type and with whom)
- ☐ substance use
- ☐ criminal record
- ☐ expectations regarding personal, financial, and social benefits of working
- ☐ money management skills
- ☐ income and benefits (Social Security, medical insurance, housing assistance)
- ☐ daily activities and routines
- ☐ regular contacts
- ☐ family members' work history
- ☐ preferences and skills for getting along with other people, working in a group, working with the public
- ☐ physical health and stamina
- ☐ personal appearance
- ☐ supports
- ☐ interpersonal skills

Mental Illness Management

- ☐ diagnosis
- ☐ symptoms and coping strategies
- ☐ medication management and medication side effects

Networking Contacts for Job Search

- ☐ family
- ☐ friends
- ☐ previous employers
- ☐ previous teachers
- ☐ community contacts

In creating a career profile, remember that the goal is to work with the strengths, life situation, challenges, and personal styles a person has, rather than trying to change the person to fit into certain jobs. For example, a person who isn't attentive to personal grooming may want to try an outdoor job setting such as a plant nursery or a recycling center rather than an office. An individual who likes to be physically active might try a delivery job or some other outdoor job. The job should match who the person is.

If someone hasn't worked for many years, has a criminal record, or has some other barrier, it can be intimidating to think about helping that person find a job. Sometimes employment specialists encourage clients to take whatever job clients can find to build a work history. This sounds sensible, but the reality is that such an approach doesn't work. People don't stay on jobs that don't interest them, and then the job search has to start all over again. Try to take the long view and help people find jobs that are good matches.

Gathering Information from Multiple Sources

Much of the information for the profile will come directly from conversations with the client. But employment specialists should seek information from other sources, as well. You wouldn't want to ask the client all the questions needed to fill in the profile (see the list above); doing so would likely irritate any person. By looking in the person's mental health record, the specialist can gain some information about the person's symptoms and current treatment. Mental health practitioners will likely have additional information about the person's illness, substance use (if any), and living situation. Further, mental health practitioners may have knowledge of the person's work history and be able to offer valuable information about the experience. With permission, the employment specialist can help the client obtain an accurate copy of his or her criminal record, if any. Finally, family members often have useful information about the person's past work and school experiences, as well as thoughts about good job matches, further education, and so on.

Employment specialists must always ask clients for permission before contacting their family members and should include clients in any meetings with the family so they don't feel that others are talking about them behind their backs. Later in this chapter (see page 53) you'll find more information about including family members in the employment plan. See the CD-ROM for an informational handout about Supported Employment that can be given to family members.

Example:

FAMILY MEMBERS PROVIDE HELPFUL INFORMATION

When an employment specialist was getting to know her new client, Wayne, she asked him which family members he would like to involve in his employment plans. Wayne said he would like to include his parents, so the employment specialist set up a meeting for the four of them. During the meeting, Wayne's parents talked about their son's most recent attempt to work. They were regular customers at the store where their son worked, and after he was fired, they asked the store owner why their son had been let go. The owner said that their son had a hard time following directions and seemed to ignore feedback about his performance. The family had seen similar problems at home—they reported that sometimes Wayne just didn't seem to hear them, even when he answered "Okay." This information helped the employment specialist recognize the importance of developing job supports to help Wayne process and remember instructions from his future employer. For instance, she thought she might suggest that the employer ask Wayne to repeat instructions in order to double-check that Wayne understood what he was supposed to do. She also thought she might offer to go to work with Wayne for at least the first week to help him learn the job. Finally, she talked to Wayne about which types of jobs he preferred, and he liked her idea of looking for jobs that have routine duties.

As mentioned earlier, it isn't a good idea to use the career profile form as a questionnaire. In other words, we don't recommend sitting with a client and asking question after question while you fill in the answers. We also don't recommend giving the form to clients and asking them to fill it in. Instead, talk to your clients about their work history, education, preferences for work or school, and so on. You could ask if it is all right to take a few notes while the person is talking, but try to spend most of the conversation making eye contact and allowing the conversation to flow in a natural way. Remember, one of the goals of working on the profile is to develop a relationship. Also remember that you don't have to fill out the entire profile in one meeting. In most cases, you will want to spend two or three meetings getting to know the person and gathering information that can be added to the profile.

After a person has been working or attending school, it is important to update the profile with each new job and education experience. Think about how much you learn about clients when you see them try a job. Now think about the next employment specialist who will work with this person. It's unlikely that this person will find your progress notes about the client's work or school experiences in a thick chart. But by adding a short update to the career profile, any practitioner can quickly get a sense of the person's work and education history, including things that worked and didn't work for that person. The CD-ROM includes a few simple forms that can help you update the profile: Job Start Report, Job Ending Report, and Education Experience Report.

Meeting Outside the Office

Meeting clients outside of the office is a great way to get to know them better. One employment specialist spoke about going to meet with a client in his home for the first time. She said that when she saw him chatting with his girlfriend and feeding the cat, he seemed like a different person than when he was at the center. The emphasis wasn't on his mental illness when he was at home.

Sometimes people are not sure what type of work they would like. An employment specialist we know handled this by taking walks with clients through the business district to initiate conversations about different businesses and jobs. Seeing people working inspired her clients to talk about what they liked and found interesting. One person showed great interest in a toy store and ended up working there.

Make sure to conduct community visits in a respectful manner. For example, suggest some possible meeting places and ask clients if any of those places sound good. Some clients appreciate the convenience of meeting at their homes, while others would prefer a coffee shop, the library, or a walk around town. If you are meeting at someone's home, make sure to schedule the appointment in advance— stopping in without an appointment is intrusive and disrespectful.

Connecting Clients to a Benefits Planner

Fear of losing benefits, especially health insurance, is a common reason that people are reluctant to consider employment. They may have valid concerns about losing benefits and then losing a job. Many times, however, clients do not have enough information about benefit eligibility to make wise decisions concerning work. *It is critical that clients be given accurate information and be helped to understand exactly how their benefits will be affected if they start working.*

Clients need this benefits information when starting to consider going to work. Some people will plan to work part time so that they can keep their benefits and may not be able to truly commit to an employment plan until they are sure that working won't make them lose benefits. Others will want to make plans to exit Social Security without developing an overpayment situation.

Trained benefits planners have comprehensive information about benefits and work incentives, including the following:

- ☐ Impact of earned income on Social Security (such as Social Security Income or Social Security Disability Insurance)
- ☐ Trial Work Period (SSDI only)

☐ Continuing Disability Review (CDR) (SSDI and SSI)

☐ Substantial Gainful Activity (SGA) Determinations

☐ Cessation Month and Grace Period

☐ Extended Period of Eligibility (EPE)

☐ Extended Period of Medicaid Coverage Rules

☐ Unsuccessful Work Attempt

☐ Expedited Reinstatement (EXR)

☐ Impairment-Related Work Expenses (IRWE) (SSDI and SSI)

☐ Plan for Achieving Self-Support (PASS) (SSDI and SSI)

☐ Medicaid D Pharmacy Program and Low-Income Subsidy

☐ Medicaid Buy-In

☐ Employer Subsidies

☐ Section 301 (continued payments under a Vocational Rehabilitation Plan)

☐ Medicaid Cost-Sharing Programs

☐ Reporting Requirements

☐ Student Earned Income

☐ Continued Medicaid under 1619(b) provisions where applicable (SSI)

☐ Resource Limits (SSI)

Further, benefits planners must be aware of local rules regarding benefits other than Social Security, for example, housing programs, food stamps, or benefits received by spouses or dependent children. It is important to provide accurate information about *all sources* of income, including retirement benefits from previous employers or veteran's benefits.

Family members may also be affected by a return to work. For instance, if a client has a spouse who receives benefits, that spouse's benefits may also be affected by the client's return to work. The benefits planner must investigate the big picture.

The rules related to benefits are extremely complicated. Don't give out any information unless you are positive you are right. If you will be counseling clients on this subject, you must stay up-to-date about benefit rules and must also help clients understand their specific circumstances. You must know the agencies that disperse benefits and assist each client step-by-step through the process, doing everything possible to help the client understand how working will affect their benefits.

Also remember that some people with severe mental illness have cognitive problems. If you are working with someone who has difficulty processing or remembering information, don't send that client to meet with a benefits counselor alone. Rather, accompany the person yourself or arrange for a family member or case manager to attend the appointment. If the benefits counselor does not routinely provide written information about the person's individual circumstances, help the client take notes. Review the information with the client later so he or she remembers and understands how benefits will be affected by work; also review what the client's total monthly income will be while working.

Because the rules are complicated and change frequently, it's ideal to have ready access to a benefits specialist—a person with up-to-date knowledge of benefit regulations who can calculate exactly what will happen to benefits if a client works a certain amount at a certain wage. Benefits specialists are often available through the office of Vocational Rehabilitation. Some mental health agencies hire benefits specialists who explain to individual clients how their particular package of benefits will be affected by working. Another resource may be Work Incentives Planning and Assistance (WIPA) projects, available in many areas to help people understand how Social Security benefits would be affected by work. To find out if there is a WIPA near you, go to https://secure.ssa.gov/apps10/oesp/providers.nsf/bystate.

Remember also that benefits planning is not a single meeting. As people continue to work, their hours may change or their wages may increase. Sometimes people forget the information that they heard earlier and don't realize how job changes may suddenly affect their benefit situation. Help clients access benefits planning every time they have a change in jobs, working hours, or rate of pay.

Discussing Self-Disclosure

During the first few meetings, the employment specialist and client talk about the idea of explaining a disability to prospective employers. This is personal information, so people should feel free to choose the option that feels most comfortable.

There are some pros and cons to disclosure. People need time to think through both sides of the issue. Reasons to disclose, or not disclose, vary from person to person. Here are some sample reasons for disclosing and for not disclosing:

Reasons a person might self-disclose

➡ So the person could ask for job accommodations in advance

➡ So the person wouldn't have to worry about hiding symptoms while at work

➡ Because advocacy from the employment specialist might speed up finding a job

Reasons a person might not self-disclose

➡ Some employers don't understand mental illness and probably do discriminate

➡ Some people don't want to focus on illness when getting a job and moving on with their lives—they try to focus on positives

➡ Some people are able to advocate for themselves

Although you may have your own opinions about the usefulness of disclosure, remember to focus on helping clients make their own decisions about this issue. IPS supported employment uses the philosophy that it's best to help people think through issues and make their own decisions because each person is the best expert for what works in his or her own life. So, rather than explaining the possible advantages or disadvantages of disclosure from your point of view, try to help clients think about possible pros and cons from their own perspective. One way to do this is to pull out a piece of paper and prompt the person to make two lists, pros and cons. For example, "So, Eileen, what do you think some of the advantages would be to having me approach employers on your behalf?" Give the person time to think. Ask "what else?" before working on the "cons" column. Another option is to use the disclosure worksheet (Plan for Approaching Employers/Disclosure Worksheet) found on the CD-ROM.

Employment specialists should answer clients' questions about employers in an objective manner. For instance, "It's true that some employers might discriminate against a person who was getting help from a program. And it's hard to predict which employers might feel that way. On the other hand, I've met employers who had family members with mental illness or who were just happy to hear about a good worker."

Some clients will decide that they do not wish to share any information about their disability to employers. When that happens, employment specialists would not be able to describe their role to employers honestly and, therefore, would try to help the person find a job in other ways without revealing their presence in the client's life, for example, by looking for job leads, helping with applications, or creating résumés. In other situations, clients will decide that they would like the employment specialist to advocate on their behalf with employers. In still other cases, employment specialists can learn about local businesses without advocating for an individual who does not wish to use disclosure. Further, employment specialists should let their clients know that they can change their mind about disclosure at any time. For example, if a client who does not wish to self-disclose to potential employers begins to feel frustrated that his job search is not yielding results, he might change his mind and ask the employment specialist to contact employers. It's also possible that a client could begin working without using disclosure and then experience problems on the job. At that point, the employment specialist should offer to introduce himself or herself to the employer to ask for job accommodations and support. See chapter 5 for more information.

When clients choose to disclose, employment specialists should discuss the specific information that they would share with employers. Many individuals would not feel comfortable sharing information about their diagnosis, hospitalization history, and so on, and this information is unnecessary for employers. Employers only need to know information that is pertinent to the job. For example, an employment specialist might say, "I could tell employers that I work for Walter Mental Health Center and that I help people who want to get back to work. At some point, I would also mention that I know someone who has experience working on cars and who is looking for a job. I would also say that I know you are a very reliable person. If the employer asked why you go to a mental health center, I could answer that you've participated in treatment and you are ready to go to work. I might also mention that you might have some difficulty with concentration and feeling nervous when you start the job, but that after a few weeks, I'm sure that you would do just fine. How does that sound to you?"

Sometimes potential employers who hear such information follow up by asking very specific questions about why the person has been out of work or is in treatment. When this happens, don't compromise your agreement with your client. One strategy to deal with the situation is to suggest that you and the client come in to meet with the employer so that the job applicant can personally answer those questions. If the employer agrees, help the client prepare for the meeting by role-playing possible responses and emphasizing strengths. Even if the employer has some initial concerns, the face-to-face meeting may result in a job.

Some employment specialists suggest another approach to disclosure in which they tell employers that they work for an employment agency and avoid mentioning mental health issues altogether. We do not support this approach. It is possible that an employer will someday find out where you actually work or that you work to help people who have had psychiatric disabilities. At that point, the employer may wonder why you were not honest from the beginning. Even if you believe that your client will not need any accommodations due to mental illness, we think the professional approach is to be up front about who you are and where you work. If your client is not comfortable with this, you can offer to help with the job search in other ways (see chapter 5).

Having an employment specialist talk to an employer about a disability could be helpful for clients who need an accommodation from the employer. A job accommodation is usually thought of as a change to the work environment or the way the work is performed. Below are sample job accommodations:

- An employer agreed to color-code salad dressing containers because the person in charge of the salad bar could not read.

- An employer agreed to give an employee a little extra time to complete the job duties.

- An employer agreed to help with *job carving*. In this situation, a person was working in a bicycle shop and did a great job of repairing bikes but did not interact well with the customers. The boss agreed that the employee could stick to working on bikes and co-workers would help the customers.

- An employer agreed that a worker could wear headphones so that the noisy work environment wouldn't distract him.

- An employer agreed that a new employee could retake a training orientation test twice because the person was having problems with concentration.

If people with disabilities feel capable of doing a job without accommodations, they are not required by law to discuss their disability with employers prior to being hired. Because many clients choose jobs based on their strengths, they have the option not to disclose. If clients start working and then discover that they do need an accommodation after all, it's okay to ask for an accommodation at that point. While employers are not required to make an accommodation, if the accommodation isn't too difficult or expensive, many employers will try to be flexible in order to keep a good employee.

Including Family Members

Often, working with a client means working with the client's family as well because they make decisions together or because the individual is dependent on family in some way. Many family members can be influential and play a significant role in supporting the client's work efforts. Families can provide information around the family member's coping strategies, interests that may relate to jobs, and employer contacts. Even if family members have concerns about the person returning to work, the employment specialist should try to develop a working alliance with the family.

Families can include parents, siblings, adult children, spouses, partners, and so on. For some people, a clergy member or close friend may be the person that they identify as their best supporter. Allow each client to select the person or people that he or she would like to be involved in the plan.

Ask other team members if anyone has had contact with the family (or a significant other) and coordinate communication. Then, don't wait to stumble across family members in the waiting room. Once you are sure that you have the client's consent, pick up the phone and reach out to the support person identified by each client. You might set up a meeting by saying something like, "Hi! My name is Laura Miller, and I am an employment specialist at XYZ Agency. Caleb indicated that he is interested in going to work. We were hoping that we could set up a meeting to talk about his employment plan and hear your thoughts." You should also ask the family where they would like to meet. Some families would find meeting at their home most convenient, while others would be more comfortable coming to your agency.

If you haven't had training or experience working with families, ask for help from other members of the treatment team. It's possible that a case manager or someone else could accompany you on your first family meeting.

When you talk to your clients about including their families in their employment plans, make sure that the clients feel comfortable and in control. Discuss the issues that you might talk about with the family in advance. Ask your client what he or she would like to talk about in the meeting, and whether there are any subjects to avoid. Finally, make sure to include your client in the meeting. Ultimately, the employment plan belongs to your client. If family members do not agree with your client, you must follow your client's wishes. Including the person in the meeting sends a message that the client is in charge of the plan, even when family members participate by sharing their opinions and observations.

When you meet with the family, be honest and respectful. Remember that most families have provided support to the person much longer than any professionals. They may not always have been treated with respect by mental health professionals, may not have been included in the process, and may even have been blamed for problems. Remember that they love their relative and that they want to help, even if they aren't sure how to be helpful. Consider what it would be like if you had a child or sibling with a serious illness. Empathy and respect for the situation that families are in and for the difficult experiences they may have had in the past can help you develop a positive relationship with families.

Understandably, some families have concerns about employment, stress, benefits, and health insurance. It's important to hear their concerns and address them as honestly and fully as you can. Only provide information that is accurate. If you don't know an answer to a question, tell the family that you will research the correct information and get back to them.

Remember that families can help you do your job. Meeting with the family provides an opportunity to learn more about the client as a worker. They can answer questions such as the following: What were his interests before he became ill? How does he enjoy spending his time now? What is his most active time of day? Families may also have resources in terms of supports and job networks. Be sure to ask if the family has ideas about jobs and about supports. They may know someone who can drive their relative to work or make a connection regarding a job. You may not learn this unless you ask.

On the other hand, don't ask family members to nag the person to go to work or to show up for your appointments. The employment plan should not become a source of conflict for the family. Instead, ask the family to point out accomplishments as they observe the person achieving small successes. For example, "Ahmad sometimes feels discouraged because he hasn't found a job yet. You've told me you're impressed that he is trying. If you think of it, could you mention that to Ahmad sometime?" Pointing out accomplishments is one way for family members to support the employment plan without damaging their relationship with the person.

Families can help with the employment process and often appreciate the opportunity to be involved. On the next page, one father describes his experiences with the VR counselor and employment specialist who helped his son.

■ ■ ■

Our son worked with a VR counselor (Jessica) and an employment specialist (Roberta). It was very productive. They made a big difference in his life. He's worked at a few jobs over the past year and is planning to go to community college this fall.

Initially, he wasn't sure whether he wanted to pursue work or school. When he felt like he didn't want to do something, we encouraged him to give it another try. We helped him manage his anxiety. The first couple of jobs that he got were not a great fit for him. When he felt frustrated, we tried to help him see that he would have many jobs in his life. We also encouraged him to talk to Roberta before quitting a job. We were able to share information about our son, who he is, his concerns, and his disability. Eventually, our son became more comfortable working with them, and during the last few months, we haven't had to communicate with them.

Roberta and Jessica were very professional. They returned emails and phone calls right away. We appreciated the way that we were able to work with them as a team to help our son. It was an extremely positive experience.

Never avoid meeting with family members because you've heard that they don't support the employment plan. Family members can have a significant impact on the plan, whether or not you involve them. For example, one team described a client named John who had been trying to find a job but had trouble staying motivated to work. John's mental health practitioner mentioned that his family was concerned about how working could affect his benefits because they depended on his contribution to the family income. The employment specialist was initially frustrated and did not want to meet with John's family. However, the team decided that the meeting would be in the best interest of their client. The employment specialist, case manager, client, and family met to discuss the employment plan. It was clear that the family did not fully support the plan, but the specialist thanked them for meeting with her and sharing their opinions. She said that she hoped that they could continue to communicate because she knew that they loved John and wanted what was best for him. After John was working for a while, the family saw that work helped him feel better and eventually agreed that they were glad he was employed.

An employment specialist on another team talked about a client who was close to his mother, who had a grave illness. He had begun to miss work because he wanted to visit his mother in the hospital. The employment specialist and client met with the mother so that she could tell her son that it would be okay if he visited her after he finished his work shift. She told him that she was proud that he was working and didn't want him to lose his job.

As you begin to work with family members, you will likely hear about the National Alliance on Mental Illness (NAMI), which is an advocacy organization with state chapters and national leadership. Family members, individuals with mental illness, and others join NAMI to learn more about mental illness, to advocate for better laws affecting people with mental illness, to advocate for better treatment and more research on mental illness, and to fight stigma against people with mental illness. If you would like to learn more about NAMI, or mental illness and treatment for mental illness, go to www.nami.org. You could also attend a local NAMI meeting to see what it is like.

Maintaining Engagement

If a client begins to miss appointments or appears to lose interest in seeking work, the team and the employment specialist need to reassess the employment plan. What has happened? Has the person become fearful about work? Is the person simply forgetting appointments? Is the person discouraged by how long it is taking to find a job? Has the team strayed from the client's preferences and goals?

When a client shows signs of dropping out, or doesn't follow through with a referral, the employment specialist works with the mental health treatment team to learn what is happening. An outreach plan could include telephone calls, home visits, or coordination with case management appointments. Below is a list of outreach strategies. Employment specialists we know helped us rank these strategies from most effective to least effective.

1 Touching base with the person during the next case management or therapist appointment. For instance, attending the last ten minutes of an appointment with a case manager.

2 Talking to the mental health team to see if they know why the person is missing appointments.

3 Making a home visit.

4 Finding out when the person has an appointment with his or her psychiatrist or medication prescriber and looking for the person in the lobby before the appointment.

5 Contacting family members, if the person has given permission.

6 Making phone calls (less effective).

7 Sending appointment letters (least effective—some people don't read all of their mail).

Learning what has happened can be difficult, especially with clients who are private or less assertive. Some people who have difficulty with relationships have a hard time explaining their feelings. The entire team needs to work together to find out what has changed so the plan can be modified to reflect what has happened. It's possible that the psychiatrist or case manager can talk to the client to find out why the person is backing off.

When the employment specialist does get in touch with the client, it's critical that the specialist doesn't show frustration about the missed appointments. Think about it from the client's point of view. Would you want to meet with someone who was frustrated with you? Someone who was pressuring you to do something that you weren't sure about? Or would you be more likely to try to avoid that person? Keep in mind that if clients are made to feel guilty or irresponsible, they will be more likely to miss future appointments. Instead, express pleasure at seeing the person again and try to learn what is interfering with the person's work goals.

In IPS programs, practitioners *don't* say things like, "If he doesn't show up for my appointments, he won't show up for work." Or, "I'm not going to work harder than she does." The employment specialist and mental health treatment team continue to help the person with work despite problems. For instance, if someone is missing appointments, an employment specialist might try picking the person up at his or her home or providing reminder phone calls rather than assuming that the person isn't motivated. The employment specialist would also talk to the treatment team, and possibly the client's family members, to try to find out how to better tailor services for that person. Questions could include "Is the person focused on another situation in her life? Having trouble with child-care arrangements?" The team can work together to help the person with these obstacles.

Talk to the mental health treatment team about whether or not the person might be having trouble remembering appointments, possibly due to cognitive impairment. If so, consider some of the strategies below:

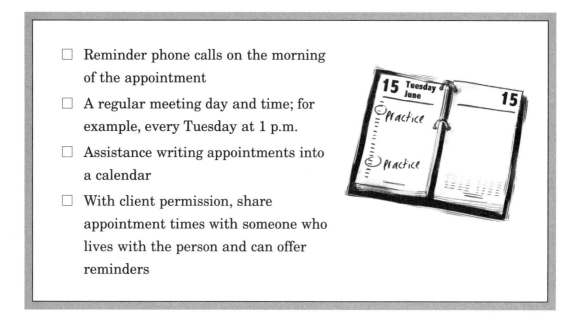

- ☐ Reminder phone calls on the morning of the appointment
- ☐ A regular meeting day and time; for example, every Tuesday at 1 p.m.
- ☐ Assistance writing appointments into a calendar
- ☐ With client permission, share appointment times with someone who lives with the person and can offer reminders

Sometimes, people do not maintain their initial level of motivation for a job. When this happens, it is important not to push the person toward a job. The natural reaction to being pushed is to push back! Try to remember the last time someone nagged you to do something like save money, lose weight, or stop smoking. You may have realized that they were right, but chances are that pressuring you to change was not effective. If someone appears to be losing interest in work, don't push or cheerlead. Instead, remember that it is the client's life, and the client needs to make his or her own decisions. You can help the person by saying something like, "It's up to you. I believe that you can find a job and that you will be a good worker. But, only you will know when it is the right time for you to work." You could also offer to help the person think through the possible advantages and disadvantages of going to work by making two lists. But remember not to push your own opinions here. The goal isn't to talk the person into getting a job. Instead, the goal is for the person to make a decision based on what he or she believes is best.

Finally, remember that in our approach clients are not closed from IPS programs due to missed appointments. If the team believes that clients may still be interested in work, they try to help them decide on their goals. Rather than demand that clients prove their readiness by following through with every detail of the employment plan (such as never missing appointments), employment specialists simply try to help their clients. Even while clients are experiencing problems, the team looks for positives and tries to help them build on their successes.

Conducting a Work-Based Assessment

Earlier, we mentioned that a good job fit isn't only related to the type of work a person does. The job environment or type of supervision can make all of the difference for some people. For example, a woman who worked in the medical billing department of a hospital found that she had difficulty keeping all of the medical codes straight, even though she was able to do that before her illness. However, a similar position in a podiatrist's office was a much better fit. The number of codes was much smaller since the doctor had a specialty. Further, there were a small number of employees in the office and it had a family feel, as opposed to the large, institutionalized hospital.

We also mentioned that vocational evaluations, work adjustment activities, and job tryouts do not accurately predict employment success for people with mental illness. This makes sense if you think about it, as the number of variables in a job are immense. For example, how could a vocational test predict that someone would get a great boss who gives lots of encouraging feedback, or that once hired, a person would decide to take his or her medication more often because he or she was motivated to do well at work?

Instead of traditional evaluations, IPS offers clients the opportunity to try working in a regular job. People often have more incentive to try hard in a real job rather than a job in an artificial setting. And even if the first job doesn't work out, it's a chance for the person to learn more about the job factors that are important for him or her.

Some employment specialists express concerns about this rapid approach to employment. Specifically, they worry that they might be setting up clients for failure or that they might burn bridges with area employers. With regard to setting clients up for failure, it's understandable to want to see things go well for clients. But remember that practitioners don't want to take on a parental role for adult clients. Instead, the goal is to help people as they take on new challenges. Most people want regular jobs in the community, so that's what the focus should be. Further, everything that happens to clients isn't just because they have a mental illness; lots of people without mental illness lose jobs, too. The more we try to protect people, the more they become dependent on the system. And the more practitioners help people become independent, the more they will make good choices for themselves and feel empowered. The role of practitioners is to support their clients' efforts and goals.

Burning bridges with employers is a fear that can be avoided by providing quality follow-along services for the duration of the job. Employers understand that not everyone they hire is going to work out. It doesn't just happen when they hire people with mental illness—it happens often! What they don't understand is being abandoned by the employment specialist. Employment specialists should make sure to keep in touch with employers (with client consent) so that the employer has someone to talk to if a problem with the client starts to emerge. And if job loss occurs, get in the car and go see the employer *that day* to express your regret. If you follow these practices, you may still lose an occasional employer, but you'll find that most employers are willing to work with you again.

Some of the factors people may want to consider about a job include the following:

Co-workers

- ☐ How many co-workers are there?
- ☐ How near to each other do employees work?
- ☐ What are the implicit social and interpersonal requirements in this work setting?
- ☐ Do employees interact with each other, have breaks together, or get together after work?
- ☐ Is it a work setting in which people go out for drinks after work or is it a workplace that has a reputation for drinking/drugs on the job?

Supervisor

- ☐ What is the nature of supervision?
- ☐ How much and how often is supervision given?

☐ Is the gender of the supervisor an issue for the client?

☐ What is the personality style of the supervisor?

Work schedule

☐ What are the work hours: time of day, number of hours, days of the week?

☐ Is there flexibility for time off?

☐ Are sick leave, holidays, and personal time included?

Work environment

☐ What are the characteristics of the job setting (for example, outside/inside, artificial lighting, noisy/quiet, hot, crowded spaces, isolated, smelly)?

☐ What types of job stress might workers experience there?

Wages

☐ What are the wages and payment schedule?

☐ How will wages affect benefits (Social Security, medical insurance, housing benefits)?

Transportation

☐ Is transportation necessary?

☐ What are the transportation options to reach the employment site (for example, close proximity to a bus line, carpool, within walking distance)?

☐ Does the work schedule match the public transportation schedule?

☐ Does the transportation plan include going through unsafe neighborhoods?

Cognitive Requirements

☐ Does the job require significant problem solving, or is the job fairly routine?

☐ Does the worker need to attend to more than one task at a time? Does the worker need to shift quickly from one task to another?

☐ Does the position require the person to memorize material?

☐ Does the position require the ability to move quickly?

☐ Is the work environment noisy and distracting?

When visiting a job site, the employment specialist can ask for a tour of the employment setting and ask questions about various positions. The employment specialist assesses the skills and abilities required for all jobs being investigated for clients.

Duplicating this page is illegal. Do not copy this material without written permission from the publisher.

61

- What are the physical demands of the job?
- Is the job sedentary or is the person required to lift up to fifty pounds continuously, for example? Does the person have to stand throughout the work shift?
- What are the cognitive requirements for completing the job?
- Are technical skills required?
- What type of social interactions are part of the job and work environment?
- What is a typical day like for someone in a particular position?

In IPS programs, vocational assessment never ends. Each job gives both the client and the employment specialist new information and understanding about that person as a worker, which they apply to the next experience. A community mental health center employment coordinator said, "In IPS, the whole process becomes the assessment tool. Everything the client does gives more information about what he likes, dislikes, and is capable of doing."

The assessment is a process based on regular work experiences. Work-based assessment is ongoing and sends the message to everybody involved that it is a process of growth and learning rather than establishing a one-time, make-or-break job experience.

Creating an Employment Plan

Once the employment specialist and client have decided on a good job match, it's time to write down the specific steps that will be taken to find the job. Each person should have a written plan for employment that is included in the clinical chart. The client's employment plan should be specific with regard to goals, activities, responsibilities, and timelines. It has four components:

1. *The employment goals* in the client's own words.
2. *Behavioral objectives* (the steps that outline how the person will meet these goals).
3. *Specific people, services, and supports* to help achieve the objectives.
4. *Time frames* for meeting the objectives.

The plan is signed and dated by the client, the employment specialist, the mental health worker, and the psychiatrist. If there are other people involved in developing the treatment plan, they sign the plan as well.

Sample employment plan:

Person's goal:

I like to help people and I want to be a nurse. I could start as a nurse's aide like my cousin did. I've always been interested in the medical field.

GOAL	OBJECTIVES	PERSON(S) RESPONSIBLE	FREQUENCY	TARGET DATE
Mary will find part-time employment as a nurse's aide.	Mary and employment specialist will identify 5 nursing homes on the bus route.	Mary and Sue Smith (employment specialist)	Once	2/3/20XX
	Mary will complete applications at above nursing homes. (Sue to help Mary with online or paper applications.)	Mary and Sue Smith	1–2 nursing homes per week	3/10/20XX
	Mary will practice interviewing skills with employment specialist.	Mary and Sue Smith	2–3 times	2/15/20XX
	Employment specialist will meet with managers of nursing homes to learn about their business and talk about Mary's skills. She'll share that information when she meets with Mary each week.	Mary and Sue Smith	At least one nursing home manager per week	3/15/20XX
	With the help of her VR counselor, Mary will buy at least one outfit that she can use for interviews.	Mary and Bill Kelley	Once	2/15/20XX

The plan includes specific information about the responsibilities of the client, the employment specialist, and the VR counselor. It also includes specific information about the type of work the client is interested in, as well as her long-term goals. The plan could also include steps that mental health practitioners will do to help with employment. For instance, if someone on the team knows someone in the nursing home business, that person could make an introduction. Or a case manager could help the client with a laundry schedule to ensure she has clean work clothes.

What's important is that employment plans be individualized and detailed. Here's a test: Would you be able to identify each of your client's plans if their names were removed? If someone read one of the plans you worked on, would they be able to describe the person's job preferences? If not, you may want to give more time and thought to the employment plans you write. For the next couple of months, try writing plans that outline all the things you and the client plan to do. Writing the plan in this manner can help you and your client consider all of the possible steps you can take to find employment and may increase the plan's usefulness.

• • •

TOOLS FOR HELPING PEOPLE CREATE AN INDIVIDUALIZED JOB PLAN:

(SP) [6] Plan for Approaching Employers/Disclosure Worksheet

(SP) [7] (SP) [8] Career Profile Face Sheet and Career Profile

[9] Job Start Report (Career Profile Update)

[10] Job Ending Report (Career Profile Update)

[11] Education Experience Report (Career Profile Update)

● IPS Supported Employment Newsletter (summer 2008): Focus on Families: Go to www.dartmouth.edu/~ips. Click on "Free Newsletter," then "Previous Newsletters." Select "Summer 2008."

CHAPTER 5

Helping People Find Employment

The next step in IPS supported employment is to use information from the career profile and employment plan to help clients find a job. Some clients may wish to do much of the work themselves, while others participate in IPS programs because they feel that they need side-by-side assistance.

Basic Responsibilities of the Employment Specialist

While encouraging the client to participate in as much of the process as possible, the employment specialist should take as much of a lead in the job search as necessary to help the client secure a job. In many cases, the employment specialist will help people find jobs by

- ☐ helping with job applications
- ☐ preparing résumés
- ☐ building relationships with employers
- ☐ answering employer questions
- ☐ connecting with human resource managers
- ☐ helping people who choose not to self-disclose
- ☐ following up with thank-you notes and calls
- ☐ sharing job search responsibilities with job seekers
- ☐ finding job leads
- ☐ helping employers create jobs
- ☐ job carving
- ☐ finding financial incentives for employers
- ☐ regularly tending to job development
- ☐ helping people with justice system involvement
- ☐ tailoring job development techniques for rural areas
- ☐ refining job development skills

This chapter will provide more details on all of these activities.

Helping with Job Applications

A good job application demonstrates that the applicant is serious about getting a job. It's important that people turn in applications that are complete, neat, and correctly spelled. Many people find it helpful to work with their employment specialist on a mock application that they can copy when applying for jobs. The mock application should include correct dates, full names, addresses, and phone numbers. It may take an entire meeting with someone to help him or her track down this information, so employment specialists should also offer to keep a backup copy of the application in the person's chart. Many specialists keep a stack of blank applications in their office so they can help each person with a mock application.

Some people have trouble writing clearly and neatly. An erasable pen may be enough to help a client correct mistakes. In other situations the specialist may actually help fill in the form while talking to the person about each section of the form and agreeing how to fill in the sections.

Online applications are often more difficult to complete because they are longer and often include a personality test. A human resource manager who helps to design some of these tests recently gave us some advice about how to take such tests:

- Remember that the tests are designed to determine whether applicants have the character traits that would make them successful in the job, not whether candidates have the correct skills. For example, the test might look to see if a person would enjoy serving people.

- Most tests look for honesty. Employers prefer candidates who are extremely honest in all situations. Further, most employers are looking for candidates who are positive—that is, people who tend to think the best of others, assume that their employer is fair, and so on.

- Test questions usually have multiple-choice answers such as *never, sometimes,* and *always.* If an applicant selects the middle answer too many times, the test becomes invalid—it doesn't tell the human resource department much about the applicant. These applications may be voided.

- If a person takes too long to answer questions or changes answers frequently, the concluding report may indicate that the person was trying to unduly influence the results of the test or may have been slowed down because someone was helping the candidate take the test.

- Try not to overthink. When people do that, their results tend to look scattered.

- People should set themselves up for success. They should take the tests in a quiet environment at a time of day when they feel fresh. It's important to have a good Internet connection. Think about honesty and being positive before beginning the test.

Regarding the online application as a whole:

- Some applications may be timed to screen out candidates who are not mentally alert.

- Most companies won't automatically screen out candidates who have a criminal history, but these applications may not be considered strong. It is especially important for the candidate and/or employment specialist to try to make contact with the person in charge of hiring.

- It is okay to log off and come back later to complete the application. Most companies do not hold that against the applicant.

Competition for jobs is stiff. Unless a client has a strong work history and looks like a great candidate on paper, following up on job applications is critical. Although many clients will not receive calls in response to their applications, you can help them think of ways to get in front of employers. For example, clients can stop by a business (with or without the employment specialist) to introduce themselves to managers. For example, "Hi. My name is John Smith and I submitted an online application for a parts clerk three days ago. I have experience working on cars and actually live just a few blocks away. I was hoping that you would be interested in scheduling a time to talk to me about the position." Employment specialists can also help clients follow up on job applications, particularly with employers they know: "Hi, Pete. Is this a good time to stop by? I wanted to let you know that someone I'm working with submitted an application for a parts clerk at your store. He actually has experience working on cars and some basic computer skills. I wondered if you would be interested in hearing a little bit about him."

Preparing Résumés

Increasingly, employers expect to see résumés along with job applications. Even when people are applying for part-time entry-level jobs, they are sometimes expected to have a résumé. A hiring manager for a national company recently explained that they hire people who have résumés because they can compare the résumé to the job application to see if information provided is consistent. Be sure to spell-check résumés and consider asking a co-worker or VR counselor to review clients' résumés and provide suggestions.

Building Relationships with Employers

Many of us began job developing by introducing ourselves to employers, talking about our program, and asking about job openings. We might have even asked the employer to interview a client who was looking for a job. From the employer's perspective, this could feel like a stranger walking in off the street and asking for a favor! A far better approach is to first spend time getting to know the employer so that you have a trusting relationship and the employer believes that you understand his or her specific workforce needs. At that point, you will be able to provide a service to the employer by suggesting a person who is the right fit for that company.

The approach that we have seen to be most successful involves a series of visits to the workplace in which the employment specialist focuses on learning about the culture of the workplace, the types of jobs at that business, and the hiring preferences of the manager(s). The first visit is to ask to schedule an appointment to come back and learn about the business. The second is to spend time talking to the manager about the business, positions, and hiring preferences. Finally, the third visit may be to discuss a person who would be a good fit for that company.

During these first few visits, employment specialists do not ask about job openings. They know that the employer will have openings sooner or later, and their goal is to develop a relationship with the employer (and help their client develop a relationship) so that when openings come up, their client can be hired before the job is advertised. Asking about openings early on focuses on the needs of the employment specialist, rather than the employer, and during this process the idea is to view the employer as another customer. Employment specialists think about how to be a resource for the employer as well as the client. Finally, employment specialists do not ask about openings during these early visits, because if the answer is "no," the conversation will shut down.

When meeting with employers, it is important to dress professionally. Think about what the people in that business will be wearing and try to match that or dress in a slightly more formal way. For example, if you are going to a human resource department of a large hospital, you would wear a suit or jacket. In most instances, you can probably get away with slacks and a button-down shirt or blouse.

Now let's review each of these visits in detail. Before meeting with employers, prepare for each visit. You'll need to know the purpose of the visit, think about materials to bring with you, and also know what you will say to the employer.

The purpose of the first visit is to ask the employer for an appointment to come back and learn more about the business. Employers are busy, and asking for an appointment is a respectful approach. To prepare for this visit, practice how you will introduce yourself and explain the purpose of scheduling an appointment.

Examples of introductions to employers:

> *"Hello. My name is Buzz Thomas, and I work for Fictional Agency here in town. I'm an employment specialist, so my job is to introduce employers to people who want to work and have the skills those employers need. Part of my job is to learn about local businesses. Would it be possible to schedule a fifteen-minute appointment with you to learn more about your business and the types of positions that you hire?"*

■ ■ ■

> *"Hello. My name is Chelsea Farmer, and I work for Mental Health Agency here in Atlanta. I'm an employment specialist, and I help people who have been out of work to re-engage in the workforce. Part of my job is to learn from employers about their businesses and hiring preferences. Would it be possible to schedule a fifteen-minute appointment to come back to learn more about* (name of business)*?"*

Many specialists believe that they can be spontaneous—that the words will come to them as they are standing in front of an employer. Having watched many employment specialists try this, we recommend practicing your introductory statement until you can say it without stumbling or becoming confused. You don't have to be a marketer to sound smooth and professional, but you do have to practice.

A few employers will turn you down, but you will find that most will agree to meet with you. If an employer says, "Sure, come back next week," try to pin the person down to a specific day and time. The appointment is likely to happen if there is a specific plan.

Be prepared to answer questions about what you do and what you hope to get out of the next appointment. Bring your business card, brochure, and appointment book. Also, because some employers will want to meet with you right then, be prepared for the second visit, as well (see page 70).

Some employment specialists ask if it is possible to set the appointment up by using phone or email. We strongly discourage this approach. Face-to-face contact helps to build the relationship. The more times that you and the employer see each other, the more likely the person is to end up working with you. Further, it is just a little easier to say "no" to someone who is on the phone.

Finally, remember that the purpose of the first visit is to make an appointment to come back and learn about the business. You don't have to sell anything or even learn about job openings during the first visit. If you walk away with an appointment, pat yourself on the back—it was a success!

SECOND VISIT

If you've been job developing for a while, you may find it difficult to avoid talking about your client or your program during this visit. But try to keep the focus on the employer, unless he or she asks questions about your program or your clients. Remember that the purpose of this visit is to learn about the employer. Your job is to get the employer to do most of the talking.

Before meeting with the employer for the second appointment, learn some basic information about the goods or services that the company produces. This doesn't mean you should spend hours researching companies on the Internet; however, a few minutes spent discovering the basics about the company can impress an employer. For example, "I saw that your mission statement is to ensure that every guest has a memorable experience. What types of things do your employees do to ensure that guests have a memorable stay?" "I read in the paper that your company is expecting to expand. Congratulations!"

Begin the meeting by reviewing who you are and the purpose of your visit. You could say, for example, "Thanks for meeting with me, Stacey. As you may recall, I am an employment specialist for XYZ Agency, and I help employers find workers who are a good match for their business. Part of my job is to learn about local businesses, including the type of people who are successful at that business, so that I can be a resource to both employers and job seekers. That's why I'm here today. For example, it would help me if you could describe the type of person who tends to be a successful employee here."

Before this visit, develop a list of questions you will ask the employer. We don't recommend pulling out a long list while talking with the employer, but rather to have three or four good questions in mind. Then use your client interviewing skills. Ask follow-up questions and reflect back some of the things you hear so that the employer can explain more fully. Here are examples of questions that have worked well for us:

- ☐ What type of person tends to be successful here?
- ☐ What qualities do you look for when you are interviewing job candidates?
- ☐ What are your hiring headaches?
- ☐ Do some positions have more turnover than others?
- ☐ Is there an employee here who is exemplary? What makes that person so valuable?
- ☐ Do you have a busy time of year?
- ☐ What is your hiring process?
- ☐ What types of positions do you have here?
- ☐ Are there types of positions that I might not know about?
- ☐ What is a typical day like for a (name of position)?
- ☐ What types of skills or experience is helpful for a _____ (name of position)?
- ☐ Why do you like working for this company?
- ☐ What are you most proud of?
- ☐ So, people should start with an online application. But you mentioned that you need people who are self-starters with outgoing personalities. If you had a friend who matched that description, how would you help your friend get an interview?

Example of an employer meeting:

Alberto:

Thanks for meeting with me today. I appreciate the opportunity to learn more about your business. For instance, it would help me to understand the type of person who tends to be successful here. (Open-ended question)

Kristin:

Well, for the vending positions, I am looking for people who can work independently. They are out there on their own filling the machines. They also need to have their own reliable transportation.

Alberto:

What else? (Open-ended question)

Kristin:

They also have to be very honest. This is a cash business. And they have to enjoy working with customers. Some of the vending people get irritated when a customer interrupts them while they are filling the machines. That's not good.

Alberto:

So, you need people who are able to work independently, have their own transportation, are very honest, and like working with customers. (Summary statement)

Kristin:

Right.

Alberto:

How do you go about finding people to fill the positions? (Open-ended question)

Kristin:

I usually put an ad in the paper, but to tell the truth, it is hard to find the right person. So many people today don't seem to really care about their jobs! Even though the economy is bad, it is hard to find people with a good work ethic.

Alberto:

It's a challenge to find hard workers. (Reflection)

Kristin:

Yes. I don't understand it. Many people work for a couple of weeks then quit, or are unreliable.

Alberto:

When you are interviewing someone, how can you tell whether or not the person has a good work ethic? (Open-ended question)

Kristin:

I guess I look for a good attitude. You, know, does the person seem inter-ested in the job? Is he or she asking questions? Giving me good eye contact? If the person has been out of work, I'm interested to know the reason.

Alberto:

That makes sense. What type of education and work experience is required for these positions? (Expressing empathy and open-ended question)

Kristin:

The person must be able to read a price list and have a valid driver's license. That's about it.

Alberto:

It would help to know what a typical day is like for a vending position. How does the day usually begin for someone in that type of job? (Open-ended question)

Observe the employer to determine if the person is interested in continuing the conversation or is anxious to return to work. Also, keep an eye on the time. If you told the employer it would be a fifteen-minute conversation, stick to this time limit unless the person wants to continue talking. Avoid asking questions just for the sake of asking, as employers will sense this and may resent that you are wasting their time. Instead, focus on things that you genuinely want to know, and when you're done, ask the employer if he or she has any questions for you.

Avoid asking the following:

- If the employer hires people who have substance use problems. Almost no one wants to hire employees who are still struggling with drugs and alcohol. Your strategy to help people with these issues is to help create a plan so the person can show up to work sober (see chapter 8: Helping People with Co-occurring Disorders).

- About their preferences for hiring people who have criminal records. Employers tend to react more favorably to criminal histories when they first meet a person who appears to have the skills for the job and who can explain how they have changed their life (see Helping People with Justice System Involvement later in this chapter).

- About information that you can easily find out on your own; don't waste the employer's time.

After the employer has described what is important to him or her, you can summarize some of the things that the employer said. This will demonstrate that you have been listening carefully, and it will also provide the employer with an

Duplicating this page is illegal. Do not copy this material without written permission from the publisher.

73

opportunity to clarify issues. For example, "So the qualities that you look for include reliability and a willingness to go the extra mile for a customer, for instance, finding an answer to someone's question. You're willing to train a person who doesn't have experience if the person is reliable and is helpful to customers. Does that sound right?"

If the employer agrees, thank him or her for spending time with you and ask one final question about how you can keep in touch in the future. "Thanks for talking with me today. It was very helpful to learn more about your business and hiring needs. If at some point I know of a person who sounds right for this company, would it be all right to stop by?" You'll leave without talking about a specific job seeker or asking about openings, and this will set you apart from the other job developers in your community.

As mentioned earlier, to prepare for the visit, you should learn something about the company in advance. Bring your business card and brochure again because it is likely that the employer will have lost those things. You should prepare a statement to review the purpose of the visit and think of questions that you want to ask the employer. Finally, set the stage for the third visit. Although you will not ask about job openings on this second visit, occasionally an employer will bring up an immediate opening. When this happens, you may decide to go ahead and talk about a person who is a good match for the job.

You'll know you were successful if you walk out knowing more about the business, positions, and hiring preferences of the manager. It's that simple. You don't need to secure a job interview or even know about job openings in order to consider the visit a success. Congratulate yourself for learning about the employer and spend a few minutes afterward writing down additional notes from the conversation.

If you have doubts that employers will want to meet with you, try this approach a few times anyway. We've found that most employers are willing to have a short meeting and share a surprising amount of information about how they screen job applicants. For example, one grocery store manager told us that the first step in his hiring process is to take applicants on a tour of the store. If the person acts bored, he doesn't hire. If the applicant makes an observation or asks a question about the store, however, he sits down with the person for an interview. Next, he asks the person what "organic food" means to him or her. If the person doesn't have some basic information about this, he ends the interview. Imagine how helpful information like this would be to the job seekers you know.

If the business has jobs that sound right for someone on your caseload, share that information with the job seeker and ask if he or she would like you to pursue the employer on his or her behalf. If so, you can go back to the employer to talk about your client and some of the supports that you can offer. For example, "Zeke, I was thinking about what you told me last Thursday—about needing to find someone who was an early-morning person and very reliable. I am working with a person whom I've found to be very reliable. He has strong motivation to work, and he's also up at five each morning. I was hoping that you would be interested in hearing a bit about him so you will know if he is someone you would like to meet."

If the employer says that the company doesn't have any openings right now, ask if he or she would be willing to meet your client anyhow. Eventually, the employer will have openings and may decide to call you or your client before advertising the job. "I wonder if you would be willing to have a brief meeting with Todd even though you don't have openings. It would be helpful to Todd because it would give him a little bit of interviewing experience, and it might be helpful to you in the long run because you'll probably have an opening eventually." If the employer agrees, set up a specific date and time to bring the person in.

To prepare for the third meeting, take your business card, brochure, and date book. Also, bring a few copies of the client's résumé (don't forget to get the client's permission first). Finally, be prepared to talk about how the person's strengths will fit the employer's needs. Review your notes from the second meeting. Don't assume that you will remember everything the employer said— if you are meeting with employers frequently, it becomes difficult to keep all of the details straight. When describing your client, try to use some of the same phrases that the employer used (for example, "He's someone who is willing to go the extra mile").

If there isn't anyone on the IPS team caseload who is a good match for a particular employer, you may decide to keep in touch with that manager anyhow if you think you would like to work with him or her in the future. Job development is often about long-term relationship building. Sally, an employment specialist, describes such an experience:

■ ■ ■

I was job developing for a woman named Chantelle who has a strong desire to work, is very energetic, but is also very impatient with other people. I thought working in a kitchen might be a good fit since she wouldn't have contact with the public and her fast pace would be appreciated. But while having a second visit with an employer, the first thing she said about interviewing was that she looks for people who walk in with a smile on their face. A happy team was the most important thing to that employer. I knew then that Chantelle would not be a good fit for her business. On the other hand, the employer was really friendly and wanted to work with our program. I kept in touch with her for months until I did know someone who was a good match for the job.

Leticia had a similar experience:

■ ■ ■

I met an owner of a small restaurant in December. He was getting ready to go to Florida for the winter because his business was very slow after the holidays. He spoke a lot about his business, and I thought it sounded perfect for a client of mine who was trying to finish her GED and hoped to go back to work by the summer. This person wanted to go back to work in May or June, so I asked him if I could come back to see him again in April when he returned to town to gear up for the busy season.

Here are some ways that you can keep in touch with employers over time (third, fourth, fifth visits . . .):

- Ask the employer to meet with someone who is not a good fit for the business but who needs help practicing his or her interview skills. In this case, you are asking the employer to donate twenty to thirty minutes to help a job seeker prepare for the job search. You should plan to be present for the interview if the employer agrees. Be sure to send a thank-you note.

- Stop by with a thank-you note for the time the employer spent with you during the second visit. "Hi, Ann. I was going to put this note in the mail to you, but I was in the neighborhood and figured I might as well just stop by and hand it to you instead."

- In some cases, it makes sense to meet the next level of management. For example, an employment specialist started working with a manager of a small sandwich shop and eventually asked if the manager would introduce her to the owner of the shop. If you do this, you should send a thank-you note to both people after the visit.

- Ask for a tour of the company or factory. Be sure to send a thank-you note.

- Offer to meet with all of the managers at a business to provide a short in-service about employment of people who have mental health issues. Educate the managers about local services that are available for workers who are having mental health or substance use problems. Human resource departments are often appreciative of this type of help. Consider developing a short presentation with one of the mental health supervisors at your agency.

- Just stop by to say a quick hello and ask the manager how business is going.

- Share good news about your program. For instance, if there is an article in the newspaper about your program, stop by to share a copy with the manager. Or, if your program achieves record outcomes, stop by to let the manager know that many employers are working with your program.

It's a good idea to keep a list of twenty to twenty-five employers with whom you are trying to maintain a relationship over time. Every few weeks, review the list to see if there is someone you've neglected to visit for four or six weeks. Don't wait too long between visits or employers may forget who you are. You also shouldn't depend on employers to contact you when they have openings. Stop by frequently so you will know when the employer is preparing to hire. Finally, occasionally review the list to see if there is someone you want to remove so that you can add other promising employers.

Share your lists with the other employment specialists on your team so that you aren't tripping over each other out in the community. You can be the lead with the employers on your list, but if one of your co-workers has a client who would be a perfect fit for one of your employers, offer to introduce the employer to the other employment specialist. If you all do that for each other, your team and all of your clients will benefit in the end by a higher number of job starts.

Again, we don't recommend keeping in touch with employers through email or by phone. Face-to-face interactions are best for building relationships, and they also demonstrate that you'll be around to provide support if the employer works with your program. Instead of asking an employer, "How would you like me to contact you in the future?" suggest that you can come by in person: "Would it be all right to stop back if I know someone you might like to meet?"

Answering Employer Questions

Occasionally, employers will ask questions that catch employment specialists off guard. When this happens, just do your best to answer the questions honestly and professionally. One word of caution, however, is to never share information that you don't have permission to share. Here are some of the questions that we've run into most frequently.

Question:

Why are you here instead of the person?

Possible answer:

I help people who have had mental health issues return to work. The people I represent have participated in treatment and are motivated to work. I help them by learning more about area businesses and the types of jobs available. If I know of a business that would be a good fit for someone, I share that information with the job seeker.

Question:

What do you mean by "mental health issues"?

Possible Answer:

No one on my caseload is exactly like anyone else. For example, one person may have had difficulties with depression, while another person may have had problems with anxiety. But two things that are important to remember are that the job seekers I know are getting help—they're dealing with their problems. Also know that I plan to stay involved for a long period of time, typically a year, to provide support to the person and ensure that they are successful. I should also mention that the people I represent have a wide range of skills and abilities. One person on my caseload is working in a daycare center, another person is working in the library, and someone else is changing oil on cars. These people are performing their jobs just as well as their co-workers.

Question:

I've worked with another program like yours and it didn't work out. [How do I know that you would be different?]

Possible Answer:

I really can't comment on another program, but I can tell you that one way I believe we are different than most programs is that we make sure to learn about each employer's needs. We think of employers as our customers. Further, I stay in close contact with employers after they hire one of the workers I know; I am usually in the picture for about a year. You know, there are some employers in town who would be glad to talk with you and tell you what it's been like working with me. Would you like their contact information?

Question:

What's wrong with John [job applicant]*?*

Answer:

I know that John is okay with telling employers that he has had some mental health issues, but I'm not sure how much detail he would like me to share. Why don't John and I make an appointment to come in here together so you can ask him some more questions yourself? Meeting John might help you gain a better understanding of how he would fit into your workplace.

During your conversations with employers, avoid using terms that are familiar to people in the social service field but not to the general public. For example, instead of talking about your *client* or *consumer,* use the terms *job seeker, worker,* or *person.* Instead of explaining that someone has schizophrenia, describe how the person's illness might affect him or her on the job, if at all. Avoid jargon such as *job coaching* or *disclosure.*

Examples of how to talk about clients:

"You may notice that Linda talks to herself off and on, but that won't interfere with her ability to do the job. Furthermore, you mentioned that you have trouble finding workers who show up, and Linda is definitely someone who will show up for work."

■ ■ ■

"Bill is sometimes nervous in new situations and has trouble concentrating. However, after he gets to know his job, his concentration is fine. To help, I could come to work with Bill the first few days and give him some reminders."

Connecting with Human Resource Managers

Some managers may tell you that you must go through a human resource (HR) department, rather than speaking to them directly. This can be difficult, as many HR managers are reluctant to take phone calls or meet with people whom they do not already know. Below are some tips from human resource managers on making these connections:

- Consider attending meetings for HR groups such as SHRM (Society for Human Resource Management). Ask people in your HR department if they are members of a group like this and if they would be willing to take you to meetings. There is a cost to join the group, but you can ask if it is possible to attend a few meetings without becoming a full-fledged member. Don't expect to walk in the door and start selling your services. You'll have to take time to get to know the people in the group. Build relationships with them based on the things that they are doing. Over time, people will ask about your job, and you will have opportunities to ask if you can meet with them to learn about their corporations.

- One HR manager gave the following advice: "Be really nice. It sounds simple, but some people are pushy when they contact us. I get calls all day every day, but sometimes a person manages to work their way in because they are very nice and respectful."

- Consider bringing something to leave with the HR manager. It should be something that looks professional and includes the name of your program and phone number. For example, it could be sticky notepads with your program's name and number across the very top.

- Think about the times that HR managers are busiest. Avoid calling or visiting on Mondays and Fridays.

- Consider sharing letters of reference from other employers. For example, bring a very short letter from an employer who says you have been a helpful resource and helped him find a couple of good workers.

- Think of yourself as a job applicant as you are trying to schedule an appointment. Consider sending a brief letter with letters of reference and calling to follow up. Make sure that all written communication is extremely brief. Bullet points are better than paragraphs.

- When all else fails, send cookies. One manager reported that he usually ends up taking calls from people who send something like this, though he also said that "the best people" don't go on and on about the cookies, they just ask if the cookies arrived and then move on to request an appointment.

- Be persistent without being pushy or overbearing. Some specialists report that they were able to finally get through after many phone calls and visits. Remember to be respectful throughout this process.

- If you get an appointment with an HR manager, send a thank-you note the next day. HR managers care about this type of professional behavior.

Helping People Who Choose Not to Self-Disclose

Earlier in this manual we mentioned that some clients would not want you, the employment specialist, to talk to employers on their behalf. They may worry that employers won't hire them if they know about their mental illness, or they may not feel that it is necessary for the employer to know that they are part of an IPS program. Whatever the reason, you should respect the person's choices and offer to help indirectly with the job search. If someone has been job hunting for a few months, you could offer to advocate with employers again, but don't push. For some people it's important to do things independently.

Example of working with clients who choose not to disclose:

Jorgé:

It's been a few months since we've started the job search, and I know you are anxious to start working. Would you be interested in thinking again about ways that I can help you with employer contacts?

Will:

I just don't think anyone will hire me if they know that I come to the X Center.

Jorgé:

So, concern that employers will discriminate is one disadvantage to having me talk to employers. How about if we make lists of the possible pros and cons of having me interact with employers? That will help me understand your point of view.

If a client doesn't want to use disclosure, you can help the person's job search in indirect ways, such as finding businesses that hire the positions the person is interested in, helping with applications and a résumé, helping the person practice interviewing questions, helping the person connect with VR, or finding job-hunting clothes. In many cases, you will still contact employers on the person's behalf but without making your relationship with the client known. For example, you could offer to visit with potential employers to learn about their business and hiring preferences, and then share that information with the job seeker. In this situation, you wouldn't share any information about the job seeker with the employer, but if your client likes what he or she hears about a business, the person can go ahead and apply without your assistance. Any information you learn about hiring preferences may help the person get through the application and interview process. In some situations, the employers you meet may sound receptive to working with you. If this happens, go back to your client and share that information. Some clients may ask you to help with an introduction to the employer if they feel that a particular employer is interested in meeting them.

Example:

Jorgé:

So, you definitely don't want employers to know that we are working together.

Will:

Right.

Jorgé:

You know, there is another alternative. I could spend time visiting with employers who hire data-entry positions and learn about the qualities that they look for in job applicants. I might also find out interesting information about the types of jobs they have. I could share that information with you, without ever discussing you with the employer. Some extra information might give you an edge. What do you think?

Following Up with Thank-You Notes and Calls

Make it a practice to help job seekers follow up on all applications with a phone call or visit to the employer. Employers receive many applications for each job, and you should try to help your client stand out. An in-person visit is probably the best way to follow up, but a phone call can also be helpful.

Help each person practice what he or she will say, and in some cases be present with the person when they stop in or place a call to the manager. On follow-up visits, applicants just need to let the employer know that they are truly interested in the job and that they have strengths to bring to the workplace.

Examples of client follow-up with employers:

"Hi. My name is Harold Bingham. I wanted to let you know that I submitted an online application for a driving position on Monday. I've done some driving work in the past and I'd love to talk to you about the job."

■ ■ ■

"Hello. This is Nattie Parker. I wanted to call to let you know that I dropped off an application last Monday. I love your store and live just a few blocks away. I was hoping that you would be willing to talk to me about the stocking position."

Be sure to help clients send a thank-you note immediately (within a day) after each job interview. It's helpful to have some plain note cards for clients to use, but if you don't, help the person write a brief note on a computer. Handwritten notes needn't be long.

Example:

"Thank you for meeting with me on Tuesday to talk about the docent position. I am excited about the possibility of working at the Cleveland Zoo. Please feel free to call me if you have any other questions about my experience."

The extra effort of sending a note after an interview, or calling a manager after submitting an application, is impressive to employers. One employer told us that although he often has 50–100 applicants for one position, he always hires someone who makes an extra effort to follow up with him.

Sharing Job Search Responsibilities with Job Seekers

Most employment specialists talk with clients about things they can do between appointments to advance the job search, for instance, picking up a job application, filling out an application, or buying a shirt to wear to interviews. It's a good idea to share these responsibilities with job seekers because it can help them learn how to conduct a job search. But be sure to suggest assignments that are within the client's skill set. If someone isn't yet able to fill out a job application neatly and completely, think of something simpler, such as coming up with ideas for two places the person would like to work. Also, if clients fail to complete their homework assignments, don't assume it's because they are uninterested in work. Many people are in your program, in part, because they have difficulty doing these things independently. Make sure not to embarrass clients for failing to complete assignments between appointments. In fact, if a client doesn't complete assignments for a few weeks, you might invite the person to share his or her own ideas for homework assignments or else drop the idea for a while. If a person doesn't follow through with assignments, remind yourself that what is most important is that the client is still engaged with the program and still wants to work. Let go of any negative feelings about what the person is not doing.

Finding Job Leads

Newspaper ads can be a source of job leads. Since lots of job seekers view these ads, however, there are a large number of applicants for each position. Employment specialists read the ads daily but view ads as only one source of job leads. A better source of leads is the one that we've been talking about—going out into the community to talk with employers. Over time, the network that you build will be invaluable to you. You may also have personal connections to add to your network right now—friends and family members who are employers or who know employers.

IPS team meetings are a good time to talk about jobs that clients are seeking. Often, a co-worker will know an employer and be willing to share the lead. It may help to ask your co-worker for an introduction.

Joining local employer groups is another way to find out about jobs. Groups such as local Chambers of Commerce, Kiwanis, or Jaycees are a way to meet employers. Some towns and cities have human resource organizations that meet regularly. Ask the human resource professionals in your agency if they know of such a group.

Another source of leads is the news section of the local paper. Reading the paper will keep you up-to-date on which new businesses are opening and which are expanding. Some places even have a local business newspaper that may be available online at no cost.

VR counselors are also a good source for job leads. They often know the local employers and hear about job openings. Meet with your VR counselors frequently and ask for help with leads.

We don't recommend long hours spent on the computer looking for leads. Although you may find some sources, this technique alone is ineffective. It is much better to use a variety of sources for leads, including the networking strategies we have already described.

Helping Employers Create Jobs

Sometimes employment specialists can help their clients and employers by suggesting new positions that address unfilled needs. For example, the Program for Assertive Community Treatment in Madison, Wisconsin, developed a job by proposing that an employer create a position to distribute coupons. The employment specialist suggested this idea when she learned of a new restaurant opening. The owner was not initially interested in coupons, but after talking with the employment specialist, he decided that he could hire two people to distribute menus in the neighborhood, door-to-door, for his new restaurant.

Business owners are sometimes too busy to brainstorm new ideas for expanding or enhancing their businesses. But many are receptive to ideas that will make their lives easier and their businesses better. The employment specialist who thinks like a businessperson may come up with a creative solution for an employer—and their clients. For example, an idea for a part-time maintenance job can come from simply noticing that a restaurant parking lot is always littered with debris and that the shrubbery is in need of trimming.

Job Carving

There will be times when a job seeker needs a very specific job that may not even exist in your community. For example, a job seeker may wish to work fewer than

Duplicating this page is illegal. Do not copy this material without written permission from the publisher.

85

Example of

JOB CARVING:

Jane wanted to work at a particular restaurant because it was within walking distance of her home, but she also became nervous when she was in busy, crowded environments. The employment specialist found out that the wait staff at this restaurant took turns coming in before opening to set up the salad bar for lunch. After meeting with Jane, the employer agreed to hire her just to come in each morning and set up the salad bar. The wait staff appreciated this arrangement, as they preferred to work only when the restaurant was open and they could make tips. Jane was conscientious about making the salad bar look nice, and the employer was happy about his decision to hire her.

ten hours per week and within walking distance of his or her home. In these situations, you may try *job carving*—asking an employer to remove some job duties from one position, or a few positions, to create a new position that would be a good fit for your client. (See page 87 for another example of job carving.)

Finding Financial Incentives for Employers

At times you may be able to offer financial benefits to employers for hiring a client, for example, through the Work Opportunities Tax Credit (WOTC) program of the U.S. Department of Labor, Employment and Training Administration. A federal tax credit incentive is available to private-sector employers for hiring employees from twelve target groups that have traditionally faced barriers to employment, including vocational rehabilitation referrals (that is, any individual who completed or is completing rehabilitative services from a state-certified agency, an employment network, or the U.S. Department of Veterans Affairs). Employers must follow timelines for completing paperwork in order to receive the credit. For more information, see www.doleta.gov/business/incentives/opptax.

Federal laws relating to the tax incentive change from time to time. We recommend checking with your local VR office or looking online for up-to-date information regarding program eligibility, as well as the specific steps that employers need to take in order to participate in the WOTC.

Regularly Tending to Job Development

To achieve the best results, you will need to spend time every week on job development. Many job developers report that they must make *at least* six employer contacts each week, that only three or four employer contacts do not produce the outcomes they want. This means that in order to make face-to-face contact with six employers each week, you need to visit ten to twelve businesses each week. This is because hiring managers are often busy and unavailable to meet with employment specialists unless there is already an appointment scheduled. Reserve time each week to focus on job development.

Helping People with Justice System Involvement

Employment specialists worry about how to best help people who have had justice system involvement, particularly people who have multiple felonies. Here are some strategies gleaned from interviews with successful employment specialists, employers, and trainers that can help your clients overcome these barriers.

1. Try to obtain accurate information about the person's criminal history.

2. Help the person make face-to-face contact with employers.

3. Help the person practice how he or she will explain justice system involvement to employers.

4. Explore options, such as expungement, for people who are eligible.

First, try to get the most accurate information you can about the client's legal record. Many people are confused about what is and isn't on their record and, in some cases, the records themselves are not even accurate. If your clients are willing, you can help them obtain a copy of their legal record. In most states, you can simply go to the police station and receive an official copy of the record for a fee. However, some people don't have the money to purchase the report, and many people with records are uncomfortable visiting a police station. If the

Example of

JOB CARVING:

Ruben had not worked in many years. He wanted to begin just a few hours per week because he did not think he had much stamina for work. In addition, Ruben had a variety of problems in social situations, so his case manager and employment specialist thought he would be more likely to succeed if he did not work much with other people. Finally, Ruben loved to garden and had a strong desire to work. His employment specialist knew of an independently owned restaurant that grew its own herbs and flowers in the summer. He asked the owner if she would be willing to hire Ruben just to water, weed, and trim around the garden. The employer agreed to hire Ruben for six hours each week.

person has an open case at VR, the VR counselor may be able to help you with a background search. If neither of these options will work, you may need to rely on Internet searches. Each state has different online resources. Kristin Tracy, an employment specialist in Ohio, reports that she uses the local court Web sites and also does record/docket searches at city, county, and state levels to gather information. As an example of resources, we've listed some of the Web sites she uses:

- ☐ The Supreme Court of Ohio and the Ohio Judicial System, www.sconet.state.oh.us. Select "Clerk of Court and Case Information."
- ☐ Court of Claims of Ohio, www.cco.state.oh.us. Select "Civil Cases." Select "Case Information."
- ☐ Cuyahoga County Clerk of Courts, http://coc.cuyahogacounty.us.

We recommend talking with other employment specialists in your area, as well as VR counselors, to learn about options for obtaining the most accurate information on legal records.

Next, talk to your clients and others who know them well about the situations that led to their convictions and arrests. Were they using drugs at the time? Was their mental illness untreated at the time? Were the convictions indicative of a lifestyle that the clients led when they were younger? A "yes" to any of these questions may help clients explain how their life is different now than at the time of the convictions and arrests.

Most employers do not have ironclad policies about hiring people with felonies. Some exceptions are social service agencies, retirement homes, day cares, and airports. Many of these organizations require that the felony is five to seven years old, or have a strict policy against hiring people with criminal records. On the other hand, many other employers have hired at least one person with a felony because they believed that the person was honest about what had happened and sincere about wanting to change his or her life. Therefore, we believe it is important for job seekers to meet potential employers face-to-face in order to talk about their past. One employer echoed that sentiment: "When I get a stack of 200 applications, a person with a criminal record doesn't have a chance unless they make a personal connection. They need to make a personal appearance."

Many hiring managers simply have their own opinions and beliefs about hiring people with criminal histories. During an employer survey, some employers said that they would be unlikely to hire people with felonies. Many employers reported that they have hired applicants with criminal histories because they were honest and up front about their record and were also able to explain how their lives had changed. Over and over, employers said that applicants with criminal records needed to be sincere about their past. This sounds simple, but, in fact, many people are embarrassed to discuss this aspect of their life and try to minimize their actions.

Help clients develop a short statement to explain their legal problems. Practice with clients over and over until they can look you in the eye and speak briefly about what happened. It's important that clients can talk about their past without showing anger. They should also take responsibility for their actions. It isn't necessary for job seekers to prostrate themselves—a simple statement such as "I made a poor choice" is sufficient. A brief explanation that is matter-of-fact in tone is best. Following this, applicants should say something about how their lives have changed or what they have learned from their experience. Finally, they can say something about why they would be a good employee. To review, here are the essential steps:

1. Develop a brief, matter-of-fact statement about criminal history, delivered using good eye contact.

2. Offer a short statement of regret (taking responsibility).

3. Describe how the person's life has changed.

4. Explain why the person would be a good employee.

Examples of how to talk about criminal history:

"There is something I want to bring up. There was a time in my life when I was involved in drugs and alcohol, and I made some poor choices. As a result, I have several felonies related to drugs and one related to breaking

and entering. I've been involved in drug treatment for over a year now, and I'm committed to staying out of trouble. I want a different kind of life, and work is part of that. I would be a good worker for you because I am a mature, dependable person. I'd be grateful for the opportunity."

"On my application, I indicated that I have a legal record. I'd like to tell you about that. There was a time in my life when I didn't really believe that I had a mental illness. I wasn't taking medication, and my thoughts were racing and confused. As a result, I was in a car accident that resulted in somebody's death. I regret that incident very much, and I now believe that I need to take medication. Working again would help me feel more responsible for my life. As you can see from my résumé, I have experience changing light ballasts, making minor plumbing repairs, and running a floor buffer."

"I have convictions for sexual imposition and assault related to a situation with my ex-girlfriend. I've been in therapy for some time now, and I know that what I did was wrong. Since my conviction, I've become involved in my church and I am focused on living a better life. Going back to work is part of that—I want to support myself. If I had a chance to work for you, I would be a reliable employee because I am motivated to get my life back on track."

"During my twenties and thirties, I made some bad choices. I hung around the wrong type of people and was in trouble frequently. As a result I have convictions related to drugs, robbery, and aggravated assault. I'm older now and I realize that I can't go on that way anymore. I believe that if I don't change my ways, I will literally die. I've been trying to turn my life around by going to drug treatment groups, and I've also been volunteering at the library as a way to give back to the community. A chance for a new life is important to me, and I would try to be an excellent employee."

"I have two felonies related to theft. What I've learned from that is that I can't use drugs or alcohol—those things result in bad choices for me. I've been sober for seven months and I continue to go to treatment. I'm also working on my GED. I'm doing those things because I want to live a different kind of life. Going to work will also help me stay on track,

and I'll be a good employee for you because work is very meaningful to me. It's an important part of my recovery."

Help clients think of things they are doing that demonstrate their desire to change their lives, for example, education, treatment, volunteer work, or helping others who are in recovery. Some employers also believe that religion is an indication of motivation to change, so if a person happens to be involved in an organized religion, they might mention that as well.

People can indicate that they regret past decisions through statements such as "What I learned from that is . . ." or "I've made some bad choices." If someone has a criminal record related to sexual offenses, however, it is a good idea for the person to say, "I know that what I did was wrong." Employers seem to have extra concerns about violent and sexual offenses and want to know that the person has a new perspective. It might even help for the person to mention that counseling has helped.

While rehearsing these scenarios with clients, you will notice that some people need help with their statements. They may not be able to remember or say it while in an actual job interview. In those cases, you should be prepared to jump in and share some of your observations about the person. If someone does not want to use disclosure, be respectful of the person's choice, but remember to bring it up again if the job search lasts a few months or longer. For people who have criminal histories, your advocacy may be the difference between getting hired or not. Employers feel more comfortable if someone is vouching for applicants who have justice system involvement. If clients do want to use disclosure, consider helping them gather some current letters of reference that comment on how the individuals are changing their lives. Letters can come from treatment providers, Alcoholics Anonymous (AA) sponsors, clergy, volunteer supervisors, probation officers, landlords, counselors, and so on.

When helping people who have criminal records fill out job applications, recommend that the person be as accurate as possible. Most employers now conduct at least a cursory Internet check on job applicants and will not hire people who are not completely honest. If the background check is not completed until after the person begins work, the person may be fired for dishonesty. In some cases, applicants do not need to indicate a prior conviction. For example, some applications ask about convictions within the past seven years only. Other applications ask about both convictions and charges. You and/or your client must read the question carefully.

If your clients are not willing to be honest about a criminal history, explain that you can continue to help with job leads, to provide assistance with completing applications, to learn about employers, and so forth, but that you cannot talk to employers on their behalf. You cannot lie to employers.

Some specialists think it is best to attach a letter to the application explaining the convictions, and others believe it is preferable to write "Will discuss in interview." Whichever approach is used, we're convinced that the key to helping the person get hired is to follow up on the application and get in front of the employer. When employers are interviewed about their rationale for hiring people with felony backgrounds, they often say that they hired these individuals because they presented well, demonstrated a strong desire to work, were trying to change their lives, appeared honest or sincere, and had skills or experience related to the job. They sometimes said that they went on "gut instincts" or their "impression" of applicants. Further, a group of employment specialists with excellent outcomes for people with criminal histories said that they usually acted as a reference for the person—someone to verify that the person would be worth taking a risk. A neat and accurate application is important, but face-to-face contact by the person, and possibly the employment specialist, far outweighs strategies used to answer questions on the application.

Resources to help with the job search include expungement, the federal bonding program, the Work Opportunities Tax Credit, and help from probation and parole officers.

- *Expungement* laws vary from state to state. In some states, it is possible to have a legal history removed from the records depending upon the offense and the length of time since the conviction. Contact legal aid or talk to a VR counselor to learn more about expungement in your state. You should know, however, that expungement is a very lengthy process—sometimes a year or longer. Don't suggest that clients wait to begin a job search. Help people find jobs while they are pursuing expungement.

- *Criminal record sealing* laws also vary from state to state. Sealing a case is similar to expungement because the public (for example, employers or landlords) does not have access to the record although it remains extant. Access to a sealed record is generally restricted to law enforcement agencies and prosecutors.

- *Record of arrest and prosecution.* In some states, it is legal for employers to ask about arrests and prosecution, even if the person was never found guilty. Obtaining arrest records may be necessary to provide accurate information on job applications.

- *The Federal Bonding Program* is an initiative of the U.S. Department of Labor. This program provides bonds for *at-risk job seekers* and is a type of insurance to cover employers against dishonesty, including theft, forgery, larceny, and embezzlement, for the first six months of employment. For more information, visit www.bonds4jobs.com.

- *The Work Opportunities Tax Credit (WOTC)* is a program of the U.S. Department of Labor, Employment and Training Administration. A federal tax credit incentive is available to private-sector employers for hiring employees from twelve target groups, including "Qualified Ex-Felons" whose hiring date is not more than one year after the last date convicted or released from prison. Employers must follow timelines for completing paperwork in order to receive the credit. More information is available at www.doleta.gov/business/incentives/opptax. Be sure to check from time to time to ensure that this tax incentive is still available.

- *Parole and probation officers* can also help with the job search. For example, they may know local employers who have hired people with criminal histories in the past. They may also be willing to write letters of reference for job seekers. In a recent interview, employment specialist Andrea Wigfield of Buffalo, Minnesota, told us about her positive experience working with a probation officer in Minnesota: "We work closely with a probation officer who is great. When we have one of his clients, he wants weekly reports. In one case, he called the employer (with me) to let the employer know that he was closely involved. He advocated for the person—said he didn't have any doubts that the person could perform the job duties. I believe that helped the person get the job." Parole and probation officers may also be invited to participate in IPS program steering committees. See the appendix and the CD-ROM for more information on steering committees.

Finally, it is important to help people find jobs they will like. Sometimes, employment specialists are so overwhelmed by a person's criminal history that they encourage the person to take any available job in order to gain experience and references. On one hand, it's true that having a criminal history can limit the types of jobs for which a person may be hired. On the other hand, since it may take some extra effort to help people with criminal histories find work, you want to increase the chances that people will stay at those jobs for a while. If someone really doesn't like a job, it's doubtful that you can convince the person to stay. Also, remember that people with criminal histories have often been asked to take responsibility for their actions so many times that they may feel belittled and shamed. This is an opportunity to treat the person like someone who deserves to have good things. Let clients know that you will work your hardest to help them find jobs related to their preferences. If a few months go by and you can't find a client's first job choice, ask if he or she would like to pursue other preferences or continue searching for the first choice.

Tania Morawiec is an employment coordinator in Chicago who knows that people with criminal histories can find employment. Below are stories of people that Tania knows:

Gerald was recently released from sixteen years in prison. His convictions had been for aggravated battery and robbery, and Gerald had also been avoiding warrants resulting from drug convictions while he was on parole. When I met Gerald, he was estranged from his family, trying to stay clean, and trying to get adjusted to changes in the world since he was in prison. He found housing that was very far from things, and he didn't have a car. On the other hand, Gerald got his GED and Arc Welding certificate while in prison.

Initially, I tried to contact people about arc welding jobs, but it turned out that arc welding isn't a very technical skill and isn't in demand like other types of welding. I learned that Gerald didn't have enough skills to work at a forge. I was able to introduce Gerald to an employer I knew at a telemarketing firm that does customer service work, rather than sales. We felt that the job was a good fit because of Gerald's excellent interpersonal skills and also because the job was on a main bus route so he could get to work consistently. The employer wanted to know about Gerald's convictions, so he had to explain how he has moved forward in his life. He was humble about talking about his past, how he learned from his experiences, and how he could excel in the job. It took about four months for Gerald to find that job.

Pam has a series of convictions related to substance use. Pam felt pessimistic about finding work because of her felonies and also because she hadn't worked in a long time. She found a job at a popular sports arena in Chicago (a very popular job in Chicago). Her felony history never came up because it was more than seven years ago. The job changed her life. She is so proud that she beat out so many other people who wanted the job and who had a lot of education—she doesn't have a GED. She loves her uniform because tourists stop her and take her picture when she is around town. I think that part of the reason she got the job was that she had a very good cover letter and also because she was willing to wait in line for hours for a five-minute screening interview and was positive throughout the entire experience!

Tailoring Job Development Techniques for Rural Areas

Employment specialists who work in rural areas use many of the same practices as specialists in urban programs. However, they sometimes tailor their techniques because fewer employers are available. Julie Cadwallader is a successful employment specialist in a farming community that borders on Appalachia. Here is how she describes her role in helping people find jobs.

■ ■ ■

Being persistent and building relationships with employers is the key. In a rural county, if you aren't persistent, people aren't going to get employed. I get to know employers, and then I follow up with them on a monthly basis to remind them that I am still out there. When a new employer comes into town, I get out there right away, whether it is a business that is going to hire eighty people or ten. There aren't many employers in my county—I can't afford to ignore any of them!

When I go into a business for the first time, I try to get the name of the manager or human resource person from the receptionist. If I can't meet with the person during that first visit, I'll try to set up an appointment so I can go back and meet face-to-face with the person. When I talk to employers, I'm interested to learn about their business. I usually also have a specific person in mind. I'm looking to figure out if there would be a good match for my client at that business.

I keep a focus on the employment goal for each client. When I started in my position, I didn't realize how important client preferences are. I just felt relieved when someone got a job. But that doesn't work in the long run. Now that I pay attention to helping people get the right job, people stay in their jobs much longer. Even though there are fewer employers to choose from in rural areas, client preferences are still really important.

I talk to employers on a daily basis. You can't just talk to a few employers a week. You have to really spend some time on this. When I started this job, I didn't know all of the businesses tucked away here and there. So I just hit each section of the county and looked around. I would just walk in and talk!

In my county there are more independently owned businesses than franchises and chains. There are also a lot of small employers. They seem interested in the federal tax credit that I can offer.

I also stress that I'm not going anywhere, even after the employer hires my client. I let them know that I'll be right here. Recently I approached a company that had a bad situation in the past with another employment agency. I kept emphasizing that I would not drop out of sight. I also let them know that I am honest. I finally got through to them, and they did hire my client.

Sometimes it helps to use another employer as a reference. I met with a new employer recently who had never heard of vocational programs like ours. I think he felt nervous about working with us. I referred him to another employer I had worked with in the past, and that opened up the door. He made the call and heard good things about another employer's experience with me. It really helped a lot.

A few months ago I was promoted. Now I'm the supervisor of our supported employment program. One thing that I decided was that we all have to look professional when we go out to meet with employers. It's a bad idea to go out in jeans and tennis shoes. You don't have to wear a suit, but you do have to wear dress pants and a dress shirt. It's the same thing we tell our clients about applying for jobs.

Another struggle that we have in this area is transportation. In our county there isn't any type of bus system at all. And because it's rural, things are spread out. Very few clients live in walking distance of places to work. I try to be creative about transportation. I've contacted private agencies that do transportation such as home health agencies and senior citizen groups. It doesn't always work out, but sometimes I'm able to help clients work out an arrangement to pay a flat fee for daily rides. Other people ride bikes, ask family members for help, or save up for cars. We're always thinking about long-term transportation solutions.

Refining Job Development Skills

Over time, employment specialists are able to build up a network of employers and increase their skills as developers. The more you get out and talk to employers, the more your confidence will increase. Make plans to spend part of every day on this activity. Practice is going to help.

Here are some other ideas to help you build your skills:

- Shadow another employment specialist who is successful at job finding.

- Job-develop in pairs for a few months until you begin to feel more comfortable. Alternate taking the lead at each business.

- View the videos listed in the tool box at the end of this chapter.

- Ask your supervisor to go out with you to develop jobs. Your supervisor can demonstrate job development skills and then help you actually make some contacts.

- Talk to your local VR counselors. Most have observed many job developers over the years and often have a good understanding of the strategies that work best. They may even know some of the employers in town.

• • •

TOOLS FOR HELPING PEOPLE FIND JOBS:

- View videos of an employment specialist getting to know employers. Go to www.dartmouth.edu/~ips. Select "Resources," then "Videos." Click on the link "IPS Supported Employment Strategies That Work" and then select "Job Development."

12 Employer Contact Log

13 Sample Employer Contact Log

14 Sample Employer Thank-You Letter

15 Sample Employer Thank-You Note

Providing Individualized Job Supports

Studies of employment programs for people with severe mental illnesses show that without ongoing help, many people have difficulty maintaining employment. In IPS supported employment programs, follow-along supports are carefully planned for each person so that all of the hard work to find a job is not lost.

Some vocational programs view job finding as the main objective. In those programs, job supports are provided but are not necessarily planned based on the person's work history, current symptoms, supports, preferences, and so on. The philosophy may sound something like this: "I'm here whenever clients need me. I tell people to call me anytime they have a problem on the job. I also check on people from time to time to make sure things are going okay."

In contrast, IPS supported employment programs think carefully about what has worked for the person in the past, and what hasn't. They develop a person-specific plan based on information from the client, family members, treatment team, and others. One person with a new job may have on-the-job coaching, while another sees an employment specialist off site a couple times a week. IPS programs view job supports as a vital component of helping people with employment. The philosophy from an IPS perspective might sound something like this: "I want to help people on my caseload develop a satisfying working life. It's a long-term perspective. I realize that goals and needs change continually. Getting a job is only part of the process."

The goal is not just to make sure that the person keeps the job, but also to ensure that the job actually improves the quality of the person's life. That means employment specialists talk to clients about whether their jobs are satisfying and help make changes as needed. Employment specialists can help clients ask for new or different duties, leave unsatisfying jobs to look for better work, and/or explore options for training and school.

The Key Elements of Effective Job Supports

In this chapter, we'll review some key steps to ensure that follow-along services are effective. Effective job supports include the following elements:

1 Individualized job supports

2 Supports to employers (with client consent)

3 Appropriate intensity of services

4 Follow-along plans

5 Continuous job supports

6 Help finding new jobs

7 Career development

Individualized Job Supports

Follow-along supports are highly individualized to fit the client. In fact, follow-along can be difficult to describe because there are no limits to the types of supports that an IPS program may offer. The idea is to be as creative as possible.

You used information from the career profile to think about a job match. Now it's time to return to the career profile. Think about the person's work history. What type of problems has the person had on jobs in the past? How long has it been since the person's last job? How does the person learn best? Will anxiety be a major issue? Getting up on time? What strengths and coping skills does the person have that will help with possible problems? What are the person's preferences regarding follow-along supports? What is the job like? Has the person done this type of work before? What is the work environment like?

Below are sample follow-along supports for people in an IPS program. How many of these have you used? What other supports can you add to the list?

☐ Help reporting earned income to Social Security, human services, housing programs, and so on. Some clients may only need reminders, while others appreciate side-by-side assistance sending in pay stubs and tracking monthly earnings.

☐ Ongoing benefits planning as the person faces decisions about changes in earnings (changes in hours or pay rate).

☐ Transportation to work. Sometimes a new job is stressful enough and the person doesn't need the extra hassle of learning a new bus route. At times the employment specialist can provide rides until the client has found a long-term solution for transportation.

☐ Travel training. For example, helping someone learn which bus routes to take or accompanying someone on the bus to learn where to get on and off. Riding on the bus with someone might even help the person build confidence about getting to work.

☐ Morning phone calls to provide support and encouragement and/or to make sure the person is up and ready to go.

☐ Help asking for raises and promotions. (Or behind-the-scenes coaching to ask for a raise or promotion.)

☐ Help maintaining motivation to keep working.

- Sometimes it helps if family members let the client know that they think it is great that he or she is working. Employment specialists can ask family members to talk about this.

- Another way to maintain motivation is to ask the client to tell you, from his or her personal perspective, about the pros and cons of the job. If someone is feeling discouraged about an aspect of going to work, it's best to get it out in the open.

- Help the person develop a savings plan for something he or she has always wanted but couldn't afford in the past.

☐ Family meetings to talk about concerns or excitement about the job, or to ask for help with job supports.

☐ Assistance solving social problems. For instance, some people aren't sure how to strike up a conversation with co-workers, or other people aren't aware that they should bring food when there is a potluck at work.

☐ Help learning co-workers' names.

☐ Plan for solving unexpected problems. Help the person develop a plan for dealing with problems on the job. Who will the person turn to?

☐ Employer meetings to review the person's performance, solve problems, and provide extra feedback to the client. This includes help asking for accommodations, changes in work schedules, and so on.

☐ On-the-job coaching. While many people don't need coaching, some people with cognitive deficits find it helpful to have extra help learning the job.

☐ Peer support groups for working people.

☐ Help with grooming and dress. Talking to someone about grooming and dress may not be sufficient. Some clients might need help buying supplies, setting up a schedule to do laundry, and so forth. In some cases, you may also want to meet with a client before work until the person has the habit of grooming before work.

☐ Assistance buying tools or uniforms.

☐ Help keeping track of the work schedule.

☐ Developing "natural supports" at the workplace. For example, a co-worker might help clients when they aren't sure what to do next, or might remind them when they need to pick up their pace. Or, a supervisor might agree to provide extra encouragement.

☐ Help to find a way to cash paychecks without resorting to costly payday loan businesses.

☐ Medication adjustments to deal with side effects or symptoms.

☐ Help managing paychecks (particularly for people with active substance use disorders).

   • Setting up auto deposit into a bank account.

   • Setting up a payee.

   • Meeting the person on payday to help purchase needed items.

   • Coaching the person on a budgeting plan.

☐ Help to leave a job that isn't satisfying to the person. Assistance finding a better job.

☐ Assistance asking for time off due to increased symptoms. Help adhering to the workplace rules about calling in, bringing in doctor's notes, and so on.

☐ Help designing compensatory job supports. For example, if someone has trouble remembering things, you could show the person how to use lists. If someone has difficulty getting things done on time, you could help the person work out a system with timers that would serve as alerts that it is time to move along. Another example of a compensatory job support, noted earlier, would be color-coding salad dressing containers for a person who doesn't read.

You may have noticed that some of the items on the list would require help from other team members. For instance, the client would need help from a psychiatrist for a medication adjustment. Or the VR counselor is the person most likely to help purchase tools and uniforms. Some items may even seem like case management, for example, helping a person budget a paycheck or work on hygiene and grooming. Remember that some people outside of the mental health system can also help with supports. Family members, peer support services, co-workers, and friends may also help clients with their jobs. Talk to each client not only about the job supports that you can provide, but about the supports that others can help with as well. You might help clients identify someone at the local consumer-operated services that they can talk to about their job, or have meetings with a person's family so that they can be part of the job support plan.

You'll need to tailor your job supports for people who have cognitive impairments. The table below lists some strategies to help people with those problems. You may be able to think of other job supports based on the person's work history, feedback from the person about what has helped in the past, and information from the mental health treatment team and family members. (Remember to get permission from your client before involving employers and others in job supports.)

JOB PROBLEM RELATED TO COGNITIVE PROBLEM	POSSIBLE JOB SUPPORTS
Difficulty following directions and/or understanding feedback from an employer	• Suggest that the employer ask the person to repeat instructions back. For example, "Drew, I need you to stop what you're doing and start washing dinner plates, flatware, and water glasses. Can you repeat that back to me?" • Set up brief meetings with the employer and client so you can help the client understand feedback and remind the client about the feedback at a later time. • Ask the client if he or she would like help learning the job for a few days or longer (job coaching). • Ask the employer if you can help create a list of job duties for the person to follow.

continued on next page

JOB PROBLEM RELATED TO COGNITIVE PROBLEM	POSSIBLE JOB SUPPORTS
Problems paying attention to the job (concentration)	• Ask for an accommodation—for example, a quieter place to work or permission to wear headphones. • If necessary, talk to the employer about *job carving*—reduction of duties so the person only needs to concentrate on one or two things. • Help the person develop natural supports, for instance, a co-worker who can provide reminders to stay on task.
Slow movements and work speed	• Work side by side with the person to demonstrate a faster work speed and to provide prompts about moving faster. • Help the person organize his or her work to improve efficiency. For instance, "Instead of walking back and forth across the warehouse, take everything you need in one trip." • Provide guidelines about time. For example, "By 10:30 you should be done watering the horses." • Alarms on watches/phones can signal that it is time to move on.
Difficulty solving problems or figuring out what to do in new situations	• Encourage the person to ask questions. • Help the person develop natural supports. For example, if a co-worker is present more often than a manager, ask if the co-worker could help with new situations and questions. • Help the person develop guidelines to use when making decisions. Keep repeating the guidelines when you meet with the person. Examples: "Always stop what you are doing if a customer asks a question." "Safety is always more important than anything else." "A clean business is very important to your boss. If you don't have anything to do, clean."
Problems with memory	• Help the person keep track of his or her work schedule. • Learn key elements of the job and provide reminders. • Help the person keep a list of job tasks in the order they need to be done. • Tutor the person—for example, meet the person after work to help him or her learn a menu. • Help the person develop natural supports among co-workers or a supervisor. Ask the co-worker or supervisor who agrees to support the client to assist the person with reminders.

Supports to Employers (with Client Consent)

When clients give consent for disclosure, supports are provided not just to clients but also to employers. Employers report that they prefer to work with employment specialists who stay in touch with them after the person has been hired. Employers find it helpful to have an employment specialist to help problem-solve if issues come up. Consider the following feedback from one human resource manager about IPS supported employment supports:

■ ■ ■

The difference with the [supported employment] program is the continued support of the employment service specialist. In the past, we've worked with different organizations and job placement services. They find a job for someone and the services basically end. It has been my experience with this program that once they get a person placed, there is then the follow-up with the employment specialist. I meet biweekly with the employment specialist to discuss how things are going; what areas, if any, need improvement; or what they can do to support us, the employer. That is the big difference. That is why I think we have success with some folks. The employment specialist is another resource as far as the mental health service side and how to improve performance. That and the follow-up, I think, has been the key.

Most employers depend on the specialist to make the effort to stay in touch. A quick contact now and then can keep the relationship alive, and this may be vital if the client runs into problems down the road. Employment specialists should make a point of calling or making appointments to check in with employers on a regular basis. Be aware of the employer's time. When things are going well, employers will appreciate the contact best if you are to the point. Don't spend more than a few minutes if it appears that the employer is in a hurry.

When problems come up on the job, the key is to respond quickly. Never wait a day to return a phone call from an employer. Further, do all that you can to meet with the employer in person to talk about the issue. This extra effort demonstrates your commitment to take the employer's problem seriously.

Remember that employers are in business to make money. They may be willing to make accommodations that aren't too costly or difficult, but they aren't social workers. It's up to you to propose ideas and offer to help implement solutions. Below are examples of accommodations made by employers:

Example:

EXTRA FEEDBACK TO REINFORCE GOOD PERFORMANCE

Jan had been working at a nursing home for a few weeks and reported that she really liked her job. Unfortunately, Jan sometimes made poor decisions about how to do her work. A co-worker, who was younger than Jan, tried to help out by providing pointers throughout the day. Jan felt that the co-worker was trying to supervise her and was offended that a younger person would tell her what to do. The employment specialist met with Jan and her supervisor to talk about

the problem. The supervisor suggested that Jan should listen to her co-worker, who did have a good understanding of how things were supposed to work in the nursing home. Jan, however, would not agree to receive feedback from her co-worker. The employment specialist asked if the supervisor would be willing to meet with Jan once a week to give her extra feedback just until Jan had more time to learn her job. The employment specialist offered to attend the meetings so that she could reinforce the supervisor's feedback in between meetings. The supervisor agreed to that arrangement and Jan kept her job, although she occasionally needed help from the specialist to iron out difficulties with co-workers.

Example:

TIME OFF TO CONTROL SYMPTOMS

Carlos had been working at a factory for a year and had been doing a great job until he stopped taking medications and became very psychotic. In fact, Carlos went to the hospital and needed to take some time off from work. The employment specialist spoke to the employer (with permission from Carlos), and the employer agreed to give Carlos a couple of weeks off. After a week and a half, it looked as though Carlos was not going to be ready to return to work, so the employment specialist asked for more time. In the end, Carlos needed almost three months before he could go back to work, and the employment specialist kept in close contact with the employer the entire time. Carlos's job was saved because of the employment specialist's persistence and because Carlos had been a good employee.

Example:

NEW DUTIES TO ACCOMMODATE POOR CONCENTRATION

Steve, a person who had trouble with concentration, found a job bussing tables in a family-style restaurant. When the restaurant was busy, he became anxious and had a terrible time concentrating on his work. In fact, Steve was having such a hard time that he was taking people's plates away while they were still eating. The restaurant manager called the employment specialist saying that he would have to let Steve go. The employment specialist asked to stop by that afternoon to talk. When she got there, she reminded the employer that Steve never missed work, was never late, and always tried his hardest to do a good job. She asked if there was other work the employer needed to have done that didn't involve contact with the public. The employer thought about it and agreed that he needed someone to pick up the parking lot, clean the bathrooms, and take out the trash from the kitchen. The employment specialist offered to provide some on-site job coaching to help Steve learn his new job, and Steve ended up keeping the job for several years.

Duplicating this page is illegal. Do not copy this material without written permission from the publisher.

107

Over time, some of the employers with whom you work will begin to view you as a resource. They'll appreciate your understanding of their business and the good supports that you offer. They may even ask you to introduce them to other job candidates. Think carefully about those requests. There may be times when it makes sense to work with an employer on several positions, particularly if the business is large and encompasses several departments. But the spirit of IPS supported employment is to provide individualized job-finding services, not to encourage people to take jobs just because they are available. Therefore, there will also be times when you will tell employers that you just don't know anyone who would be a good fit.

Appropriate Intensity of Services

Just as the type of supports should be individualized, so should the intensity. The amount of supports provided will wax and wane depending on whether the job is new or whether the client has recently had a job problem. Take a minute to read the story below and think about whether or not the employment program did a good job of providing individualized supports.

On a Monday afternoon, an employment specialist reported that she was concerned about one of her clients who had started work on Saturday. The person was supposed to call her on Monday morning to tell her how the first couple of days had gone, but she hadn't received the phone call. She said that she was particularly worried because this person had lost his last couple of jobs within a few days.

What might you have done differently? Did it sound as though the employment specialist had thought about the client's job history when she was planning job supports? We wondered about the type of supports that she could have provided over the weekend. Sometimes employment specialists need to talk to their supervisors about altering their work schedules so that clients can receive the help they need *when* they need it. When a client has recently become employed, it is probably a good idea to provide supports in an assertive manner until the person settles into the job. For some people that may mean daily contact, while for others that could mean weekly meetings to talk about the job. We recommended having weekly face-to-face contact for at least the first couple months of the job.

When you are unsure about the amount of services to provide, consider offering more services rather than fewer; a few extra appointments are a small price to pay if the client is able to keep the job. After a few weeks, you may find that you are able to back off. Yet don't rely on clients to call if they have a problem on the job. Some people just aren't aware that a problem exists, even if the employer feels that he or she has been giving direct feedback. Further, some clients might not want to bother you. Instead, plan regular appointments to talk about the job, problem-solve job issues, help the person think of ways to excel at work, and plan long-term career goals.

Try to remember that working people are busy. Even if the job is for just a few hours each week, that might feel like a lot if the person hasn't worked for a while. Therefore, make follow-along supports as convenient as possible. Offer to meet with clients at their home or in a location of their choice. Also, ask about the time of day that works best for the person.

When thinking about the intensity of supports that you should offer, consider the following questions:

- How new is the job?
- What are the characteristics of the new job? Job duties? Work pace? Work environment?
- How did the person's last job go?
- Is the person having symptoms or other issues that might affect the job?
- What has the employer said about the person's performance?
- Is the person reporting anxiety about the job?
- What are the client's preferences for job supports?

Follow-Along Plans

Now that you and others have done a lot of thinking about the type and intensity of supports that might be helpful to the person, it's time to put it down on paper. Writing the follow-along plan will help to flesh out the details about who is going to do what. Also, don't forget that just like the job search plan, follow-along plans should have a lot of information that is specific to the person. A good follow-along plan should tell you who the person is even without a name at the top of the page. Here's a sample follow-along plan:

John's goal:

I'm glad that I found a job that's around cars, and I want to do well. But I wish that the job had more hours. I want to work at least twenty hours a week.

GOAL	OBJECTIVES	PERSON(S) RESPONSIBLE	FREQUENCY	TARGET DATE
John will work successfully as a delivery driver for Auto World.	John will be able to find the stores to which he must deliver parts. John's employment specialist will drive with John to each of the stores before his first day of work.	John and Gerri Smith (employment specialist)	Once	7/12/20XX
	John will meet with his employment specialist on Mondays and his case manager on Thursdays to talk about the job and strategies to manage any problems.	John, Gerri Smith, Amy Carvell (case manager)	Weekly for the first three months of work	10/12/20XX
	John's employment specialist will call him to provide support before his first day of work and also on the following Monday.	John and Gerri Smith	Weekly for the first two weeks of work	7/24/20XX
	John, his employment specialist, case manager, VR counselor, and parents will meet after John has been working for one month to discuss the job and determine if other supports would be helpful.	John, Gerri Smith, Amy Carvell, Randy Davies (VR counselor), Mrs. and Mr. X.	At least one time	8/15/20XX
John will be able to use feedback from his boss to improve his performance.	John and his employment specialist will meet with his supervisor after two weeks of work, and monthly thereafter. John's employment specialist will help him think about the things that his supervisor says and ways to change his performance, if needed.	John and Gerri Smith	After two weeks of work and monthly thereafter	1/15/20XX

continued on next page

GOAL	OBJECTIVES	PERSON(S) RESPONSIBLE	FREQUENCY	TARGET DATE
John will increase his work hours.	John and his employment specialist will ask his supervisor for an increase in work hours.	John and Gerri Smith	Once	10/1/20XX

The plan should be signed and dated by the client, the employment specialist, the mental health worker, and the psychiatrist. If there are other people involved in the treatment plan, they should sign the plan as well.

Continuous Job Supports

As the beginning of this chapter mentioned, many clients are unable to keep their jobs without ongoing support. IPS programs take this need seriously and make plans to ensure that each client will have support available for the duration of the job. In fact, a few people may stay in the IPS program for years. Others, however, will find a job that they like and settle comfortably into that job. When this happens, the treatment team can discuss who would be the best person to provide job supports. Remember that the person may also have people outside of the mental health system who can help with the job, such as family members, friends, peer support services, or employers.

The team should think about how long the job has been stable, the amount and types of supports that seem to be necessary, any changes in the client's personal life that may have occurred recently or may occur soon (such as the loss of a relationship or a move to a new living situation), and other factors that could affect the job. If the team decides that the case manager could provide supports, someone on the team takes the idea back to the client for a discussion. The example on page 112 outlines the team decision-making process about job supports.

Example of

RE-EVALUATION OF JOB SUPPORTS:

Alice had been working for a year. She liked her job, the hours, and her supervisor. She didn't have any plans to leave her job in the near future. When she started working, she had a few difficulties with learning the job and managing anxiety, but it has been smooth sailing since then. The employment specialist had even stopped helping Alice report her earnings to Social Security because Alice was doing that on her own. The employment specialist made a monthly phone call to the employer, and the employer had consistently reported that Alice was doing well. The team talked about whether the case manager could begin providing supports to Alice. It seemed that the job was stable enough and the case manager was able to provide the kinds of supports that Alice needed. For example, the case manager could talk to Alice about her job during their appointments twice each month. The team thought that monthly calls to the employer were probably unnecessary at this point and that the employer could call the employment specialist if a problem developed. However, Alice's psychiatrist pointed out that it would be summer in a couple of months and that Alice often had symptoms of mania during the summer. The team decided to wait until autumn to make any changes.

When it seems that a working person no longer requires job supports from the IPS program, the mental health practitioner, client, and employment specialist meet as a group to discuss closing the person's case on the IPS team. When this happens, mental health practitioners agree to take over providing ongoing job supports. The client and employment specialist share information with the mental health practitioner about the types of supports that have been helpful in the past, as well as information about the job, the supervisor, and any issues that have come up in the past. The discussion should also involve developing a plan for handling any job problems the client may have in the future. For example, the employment specialist could explain that IPS supported employment services will be available immediately if the client has difficulty on the job or decides that he or she would like to move on to a new job.

Most people who transition off the IPS caseload will probably be comfortable enough in their jobs that they no longer need someone to contact their supervisor on a regular basis. But, if the team believes that it is still a good idea to have regular employer contact, case managers and counselors take on this responsibility. Many of them are uncomfortable with this task because they have not received training or had experience in such work. In these cases, it helps to have the employment specialist introduce the mental health practitioner to the employer in person and to give the practitioner tips about working with that employer.

If family members or other natural supporters have been involved in the employment plan, practitioners should solicit their input (with permission) before making a change such as transferring a person off the IPS caseload. Now would be an excellent time to schedule a family meeting with the client, employment specialist, and mental health practitioner present. If the decision is made to go ahead with the transfer, family members may be able to help the person decide if he or she needs assistance in the future. Further, since the family was asked for help in the beginning, it is respectful to keep them informed and involved (with ongoing client permission) throughout the employment process.

If the person still has an open VR case when the team is thinking about a transfer, the employment specialist must talk to the VR counselor as well. These situations will not occur frequently, but there will be times that a client decides he or she doesn't want job supports during the first three or six months of work when the case may still be open with VR. This can cause difficulties for the VR counselor, so call the counselor right away.

Help Finding New Jobs

In IPS supported employment programs, all jobs are viewed as positive experiences. Even when a job loss occurs, the employment specialist, treatment team, VR counselor, and sometimes family members talk with the client about what was learned from the work experience. Regardless of how the job ended, the team encourages the person to think about a next job and offers to assist with a new job search right away. In this way, the old job can be framed as a transition, whether the client left voluntarily or was laid off or fired.

Example of

LEARNING FROM EACH JOB EXPERIENCE:

Tom was a person who wanted to work in spite of very high
levels of anxiety. Tom's first job was in a busy grocery store
stocking produce. But it was clear that he felt uncomfortable around
so many people, and after a few days, he refused to go back to the job. The employment specialist
decided he would have to help Tom find a job in a quiet environment. The next job they found
was in a greenhouse. Tom liked the environment much better but had difficulty with the work
since his duties changed from day to day. Tom had trouble making decisions about what needed
to be done and often did nothing rather than take the chance of making a bad decision. In the
end, Tom's boss let him go. The employment specialist and Tom went back to the drawing board
and tried to think about jobs with routine duties in quiet environments. Eventually, Tom found a
part-time job cleaning offices in the evenings. The job was pretty much the same from day to
day and ended up being a good match for Tom.

In this example, Tom left his first job without giving notice. The employment
specialist probably encouraged Tom to give at least some notice, but in the end he
recognized Tom's right to make his own decisions. He remained hopeful and offered
to help find another job right away. Even after the second job, the employment
specialist viewed the job loss as a learning experience and went on to help Tom
find a better match. Some clients may try more than two or three jobs, but each
job is a success because you are both learning more about what fits or doesn't fit
for the person.

When people decide to leave jobs that are unsatisfying or unpleasant,
employment specialists respect the person's right to move on. Clients are not
encouraged to stay at jobs that they don't like. For instance, an employment
specialist wouldn't suggest that the person keep a job for a while to gain work
experience and certainly wouldn't threaten to discontinue services. Instead,
employment specialists talk to the person about likes or dislikes regarding the
job. In some cases, it may be possible to ask for a change in job duties or work

hours so that the job is more appealing. But when job changes don't appeal to the client, the employment specialist will help the person develop a plan for moving on. They talk to each person about their preferences for quitting right away or keeping the job while beginning a new job search. They also provide information about how to quit a job. For instance, they might suggest that the person meet with their employer in person and provide two weeks' notice. They might even offer to go with the person to provide moral support.

In addition, employment specialists attempt to preserve their relationships with employers. When clients are fired or quit without notice, the employment specialist goes to the employer in person to thank the employer for working with the program and to acknowledge that things didn't work out.

Example of working with employers:

> *"Thanks for calling me this morning to let me know that Bill walked off the job again and that you had to let him go. I'm sorry that Bill didn't work out for this job. I thought this was a good job match, but it seems that I was wrong. I want to take some responsibility for how things turned out and also thank you for working with our program."*

It can be uncomfortable to deal with an irritated employer, but this face-to-face effort often preserves the relationship between the employer and employment specialist. Taking responsibility, even if you did the best anyone could, is a great way to preserve the relationship. Employers will respect your effort to end things on an honorable note and are more likely to be willing to work with you in the future.

Because each job provides crucial information about the client's preferences and abilities, it's also important to take time to record information about the job, and the job ending, in the client's chart. Consider the person who will take your job when you leave your position. It would be incredibly helpful for that person to have access to all the information that you and the client learned from each job. Because charts often have a large number of progress notes, we recommend updating the career profile, rather than burying the information in a progress note. The CD-ROM includes three forms that can be used to update the profile. The first is a Job Start Report that provides information about the job at the time the client became employed. The second is a Job Ending Report that provides a record of how the job went for the person. The last is an Education Experience Report that provides information about the person's experiences in school and training programs.

Career Development

Think about your very first job. Chances are you've switched jobs at least a few times since then. Chances are that you also have plans to switch jobs a few more times before you retire. Clients want opportunities for better jobs just like anyone else. Some people may want to find work that is more interesting, others might want better pay, and some may want work that is less physical as they age. Career development involves talking to people about their long-term hopes for employment and then making plans to help them achieve those goals. Some people have

---

Examples of

CAREER DEVELOPMENT:

Susan's goal was to work in an office as an administrative assistant. With the help of her employment specialist, she was hired in a temporary position at a city government office as an administrative assistant. To become a permanent employee, she learned that she would need to be proficient at Excel and PowerPoint. Susan's VR counselor helped her purchase those software programs and related textbooks so she could learn the programs on her own. Next, she and her employment specialist revised her résumé to reflect all her newly acquired skills, and she applied with the city for a permanent job. She was hired and was pleased that her new position came with private insurance. The employment specialist and Susan eventually developed a follow-along plan that included a gradual exit from the IPS supported employment program over the course of a year. After exiting the program, Susan kept in touch with her employment specialist and reported that she had been promoted again.

Lakisha had been working in a retail store stocking shelves and keeping the store clean. She liked her co-workers and the location of the store, but she didn't enjoy cleaning. Her goal was to become a cashier at the store. Lakisha's employment specialist helped her talk to the boss about a move to a cashier position, and he also provided some job coaching when Lakisha made the job change.

---

goals that are related to a change in job duties or employers, while others wish to advance by learning new skills or going to school.

IPS supported employment programs can help people learn about available GED programs, certified job training programs, and college degrees. They may take people to visit programs and talk to instructors or advisors. They can also help clients investigate financial aid and other methods to pay for school. Finally, they can help individuals access services for students with disabilities, which are

---

Examples of

CAREER DEVELOPMENT:

John's dream job was to work at the science center teaching educational classes to student groups on academic field trips. With the help of his employment specialist, he was able to obtain an entry-level job as an assistant. Working with children and school groups piqued John's interested in returning to college for a degree in education. With the additional experience John acquired in college, the science center promoted him to field instructor, and he then had the opportunity to take the science projects into grade school classrooms. When John made the decision to attend college full time, the science center promoted him to weekend manager, which worked well with his school schedule.

Fred had an entry-level job in cable communication, in which he primarily helped install satellite dishes. As television prepared to go from analog to digital, Fred's employment specialist asked him if he had thought about learning how to convert televisions. Fred decided that he would like to prepare for that type of work and learned about a weekend seminar that would provide the certification he needed. Ultimately, Fred was hired by a business with a large hotel contract to convert all their televisions.

available at all secondary education institutions. These services often include opportunities for tutoring, extra test-taking time, and other accommodations.

Take some time to visit the GED programs, vocational training programs, and colleges in your area. Talk to your VR office to learn about their experiences with these institutions and the types of financial aid that are available. Gathering even a little bit of information on these subjects will prove helpful when a client expresses a particular interest. Also, see chapter 7: Helping People with School.

The trick is knowing when the people on your caseload are thinking about, or wishing for, a job change. Some people may have ideas that they haven't shared with you, while others may not be aware that you are available to help with career development. We recommend asking clients about job satisfaction and long-term job goals on a regular basis. For instance, you could ask those questions each time you help clients update their employment plans.

Try to remain hopeful that clients can succeed with their career plans. Just as it is difficult to predict who will succeed at work, it is hard to predict who will flourish after a job change or who will succeed in earning a degree. Employment specialist Phyllis Wilcox talks about the need to put aside assumptions about who will be successful:

Our clients have been told "no" too much. I had a client with schizophrenia who wanted to attend school. Some people thought that he couldn't do it, but this client continues to maintain a 2.5 GPA as he takes the bus ninety minutes each way. He even lost his housing at one point, but he survived and he managed to keep making progress in school. So I'm not going to tell someone they can't pursue their goal.

SUMMARY

In IPS supported employment programs, follow-along supports are individualized. The type and intensity of supports should vary from person to person and should be planned in advance. Nicole Clevenger once received supported employment job supports and is now an IPS supported employment trainer. Below are some of her thoughts about the importance of providing supports that have value to the working person:

■ ■ ■

People's lives fill up when they go back to work, even if the work is part time. So there isn't much motivation to engage in follow-along services unless you feel that there is some value in it for you. You have to believe that you are getting something out of meetings with the employment specialist. Otherwise it feels like another chore—just one more thing to do.

My employment specialist did some things that were really helpful. She tried hard to learn about my job and to understand what my workday was like. She was also great at helping me reframe things that didn't go well so that I could stay positive and hopeful about working.

One thing that she did that was less helpful was to stop by my home when we didn't have an appointment. I felt that she didn't respect my time. It was intrusive. It's important for employment specialists to schedule appointments. That also promotes the idea that there is a follow-along plan—that there are planned appointments because there is something specific to work on rather than just a "check-in service."

It is good to meet people in the community. Ask the client where he or she would like to meet—their home, a coffee shop, library, work-place . . . By meeting people in convenient places, you can incorporate the follow-along into their daily routine so they don't have to go out of their way to get the service. That's supportive!

Finally, I think it's important to think about job supports from the very beginning. It can be helpful to begin identifying possible work challenges from the start by talking about previous jobs. Planful follow-along can help people avoid repetition of bad experiences. It can also help people plan for careers instead of just a single job. Both of those types of supports are value laden.

TOOLS FOR PROVIDING JOB SUPPORTS:

10 Job Ending Report to learn from each job experience

11 Education Experience Report

16 IPS Supervisor's Guide to Individualized Follow-Along Plans

17 Sample Job Follow-Along Plan

CHAPTER 7

Helping People with School

Some people are surprised to learn that supported education is a part of IPS supported employment. In fact, IPS programs have always helped people with education, though the structure of supported education services has not yet been well defined. As we mentioned at the beginning of this book, IPS supported employment is an evolving field. We don't think that we will ever say, "Now we know exactly how IPS services should be delivered." Education supports are a part of IPS that we are learning about now. We hope that, over time, research will provide us with a better understanding about how to help clients with their education goals. In the meantime, we encourage IPS supported employment programs to help individuals with education if three criteria are met:

1. *The education or training program is related to an employment goal.* For example, computer classes might help to obtain a job fixing computers. When clients wish to take classes only for personal enrichment, we believe that education supports should be provided by the mental health team, not the IPS unit—reserving the limited space available on the IPS unit for people who want to work. Agencies rarely have enough employment specialists to serve all of the people who want to work. Therefore, we suggest that capacity on the IPS unit be reserved for people who have an employment goal.

2. *The education or training program is not designed specifically for people with disabilities.* Just as IPS supported employment focuses on competitive jobs, it also focuses on regular education and training programs that are available to all community members, regardless of disability status. One of the guiding principles of IPS is that it helps people rejoin their communities, rather than promote segregated options for school and work. Further, IPS supported employment focuses on competitive jobs and mainstream school options, rather than work readiness programs, because that is what clients say that they prefer, and that is what has been shown to be most effective at helping people with competitive jobs.

3. *The person requires a significant degree of help to be successful in school.* Some clients may need only a bit of counseling support in order to succeed in school. In these situations, we believe that the mental health team can provide supports, thereby reserving space on the IPS supported employment unit for people who need more help.

Providing Supported Education Services

In this chapter, we will summarize what we have learned about supported education services to date, including

①   Staffing supported education services

②   Practicing zero exclusion

③   Helping clients select education programs

④   Accessing accommodations at school

⑤   Helping students make timely decisions

⑥   Providing other types of education supports

Staffing Supported Education Services
In some models of supported education, one person in the IPS unit specializes in this area and provides help to anyone in the unit who wants education or job training. The advantage of this approach is that the supported education specialist has time to become knowledgeable about financial aid, local programs, and services for students with disabilities. The disadvantage to this approach is that some clients may want to pursue both school and work at the same time. If that happens, a client might have to work with both an employment specialist and an education specialist. Another approach is for each employment specialist on the team to provide supported education services. The advantage to this is that one specialist can help an individual with both goals. The disadvantage is that it can be difficult for specialists to have enough time to become experts in supported education as well as supported employment.

Although research has yet to examine which approach is most effective, we are confident that supported education should be part of the IPS supported employment unit. If one person is dedicated to supported education, the person still should be supervised by the IPS supervisor and attend weekly vocational unit meetings. Removing supported education from the unit could reduce the focus on career development.

Practicing Zero Exclusion

In IPS, jobs are viewed as transitions. Just as every job can be a learning experience, experiences in school and training programs can provide lessons as well. For example, if a person has trouble keeping up with classes, he or she might decide to take a smaller course load the following quarter. We know one client who completed a one-year certification by taking one class at a time over a three-year period. Also, remember that you will be able to help clients if they experience difficulties. For example, if a person receives a failing grade on a test, you can help that person think about options to drop the course or receive tutoring (or other supports). Finally, many school programs require prospective students to take entrance exams. Some clients may decide on their own to change their education goals based on the results of these exams. Just as we don't have the ability to predict who will be successful at work, we don't have the ability to predict who will be successful at school. Sometimes personal determination makes all the difference.

You can help clients learn from their experiences by locating transcripts and reviewing grades from previous schools. Talk to clients about their educational strengths to help them decide which type of education is right for them. Also, if you learn that someone has failed a course, you can help the person find out if it is possible to retake the course and improve the grade.

Helping Clients Select Education Programs

Education experiences can include, but are not limited to, high school diplomas, General Equivalency Diploma (GED), credentialing programs or vocational schools, community colleges, or four-year colleges. The first step in helping clients select which experience to pursue is to talk to them about their educational goals. How does the education and training fit their long-term career goals? Consider meeting with a VR counselor to learn more about clients' areas of interest, or meet with an advisor from the school to learn about job opportunities related to specific degrees or certificates.

Help clients visit schools or training institutions in your area that have programs related to their interests. Ask to speak to advisors and/or instructors about the program. What is the length of each program? How much of the work is hands-on versus didactic? How many people are in the classes? Historically, what percentage of students has been able to complete the program? What are some examples of jobs that are related to the degree or certification? Help clients develop a list of questions before visiting the school. Also, give people a chance to spend time in the environment and make a thoughtful decision about the school program that would be the best fit.

Accessing Accommodations at School

Almost all educational institutions have resources for students with disabilities. The name for these services varies, but sometimes they are called Disabled Student Services, Disability Services for Students, Center for Students with Disabilities, or Disability Support Services. Make an appointment to visit with someone in this office or center at each type of educational institution in your area to learn about the services offered and to begin building relationships with people who may be able to help your clients. Some clients may not want to sign up for these services because it means disclosure of a disability. Try to understand these concerns. Is the person afraid of discrimination or embarrassed over talking about mental health issues? The individual must make this choice, but you can help by providing information about the services offered and also by helping the person think about the possible benefits or costs of disclosure. Additionally, you can offer the option of signing up for the services, but only using them if needed. In other words, the services can be a backup plan in case the person needs additional help.

When someone is having difficulty with a class, help the student think about the possible benefits and costs of approaching the instructor. Many professors want to see students succeed and are willing to help them with their course. Some professors will spend extra time with students to coach them through the course, and others may provide suggestions about how to best approach the course. Ask clients if they would like you to go with them to talk to the professor. If not, offer to practice what they might say to their professors.

Helping Students Make Timely Decisions

In general, it is best to deal with problems as soon as they arise. Students are more likely to be successful if they do not fall behind in class. In addition, if clients are having problems with a class, you should help them stay on top of drop dates—sometimes it is better to drop and retake a class than to receive a poor grade. Finally, people who drop out of school are less likely to ever complete their degree than those who stay in school. Help people think through options such as going to school on a part-time, or even very part-time basis, rather than dropping out of a program altogether.

Providing Other Types of Education Supports

- ☐ assistance in the development of good study skills
- ☐ help developing a study schedule
- ☐ assistance with school applications
- ☐ assistance with financial aid and grant applications
- ☐ assistance with course selection
- ☐ help figuring out practical matters, including transportation or child care
- ☐ help finding classrooms
- ☐ assistance buying books and supplies
- ☐ help planning where to spend time between classes
- ☐ help managing anxiety about classes or tests (mental health practitioners could help with this)
- ☐ information about effective test preparation and test-taking strategies
- ☐ advocacy for accommodations, such as taking a test in a separate location to reduce distraction or extra time to complete assignments (both may require work with the office for students with disabilities)
- ☐ help finding a quiet place to study
- ☐ medication adjustments (psychiatrist or nurse practitioner)
- ☐ help with social skills needed at school (mental health practitioners)
- ☐ strategies for symptom management (mental health practitioners)

• • •

| TOOLS FOR HELPING PEOPLE WITH EDUCATION: | 18 Sample Education Support Plan |
| | 11 Education Experience Report |

CHAPTER 8

Helping People with Co-occurring Disorders

In this chapter we'll discuss strategies for helping people who have both a mental illness and a substance use disorder—co-occurring disorders. Substance use disorders are very common among people with mental illness. In fact, the rate of current or recent substance use or dependence among people with severe mental illness is 25–35 percent.

Work can help clients recover from substance use disorders just as it helps people recover from mental illnesses. When people have reason to hope for a better life, they are more likely to focus on abstinence or reduced substance use. Some people may feel so empowered by going to work that they gain confidence that they can stop using. As one client remarked, "I managed to go back to work and that's a big step forward. Maybe I can make other changes." Other people may decide to cut down or stop using because they want to keep a job that is important to them.

An old approach to vocational services was to insist that people get sober before offering help with jobs. Some practitioners even required a certain number of months of sobriety. We have since learned that if you hold out too many hoops for people to jump through, some people will just give up on working. As one employment specialist put it, "For some of my clients, work is the only good thing they have going on in their lives. Why wouldn't I want to help with work? I applaud their grit—the fact that they are out there working at the same time they're dealing with so much." Work supports recovery from substance use disorder by providing the opportunity for meaningful activity. The work itself can be what helps a person with recovery.

Research also shows that people with co-occurring disorders can be successful at work. It seems that motivation to work often overrides the difficulties presented by substance use.

Some practitioners worry that helping people with work while they are still using substances may result in situations that are not in the best interest of their client or community. Some specific concerns and suggestions follow:

- *Illegal substance use.* We do not recommend that employment specialists condone or encourage the use of illegal substances. Rather, employment specialists should recognize that it is not their right to make decisions for their clients, and also that they do not have the skills and training needed to counsel in this area. Employment specialists should focus on helping the person with employment, while allowing the mental health team and/or substance abuse specialist to focus on helping the person with substance abuse issues. Team members can tell clients that they believe they can live a better life without drugs and also gently point out the ways that drugs are interfering with their goals.

- *Safety issues.* Whenever employment specialists have a concern about the safety of clients or others in the community, they should take their concerns to the mental health team and psychiatrist. For example, if a specialist believes that a client who is operating a forklift has had a relapse and may be going to work while high, the specialist should talk to the case manager and clinical supervisor immediately, rather than waiting for the weekly mental health treatment team meeting. The employment specialist might also include his or her supervisor in the discussion. The team should strategize options for safety that may include helping the client arrange for time off from work.

- *Job loss.* Some clients may lose jobs due to substance use, but this can be a valuable learning experience for those people regarding the ways that substance use is interfering with their goals. However, research also reveals that most people who had the most severe substance use disorders (requiring frequent hospitalizations and other interventions) were not interested in employment because they were having such a difficult time managing their lives.

Strategies for Dealing with Substance Use

Another reason that people with co-occurring disorders are successful in work may be that IPS supported employment programs use particular strategies to help deal with the substance use. Five strategies lead to success:

1. Include information about substance use in the career profile.

2. Find jobs that support recovery.

3. Help working people manage money.

④ Ask the treatment team to plan and provide supports.

⑤ Emphasize strengths and foster hope.

Include Information about Substance Use in the Career Profile

In addition to collecting information about the person's work history, preferences, and education history, the career profile can be used to gather information about substance use. For example:

- Is the person working on recovery? Has the person been abstinent for any length of time? Does the person believe that substance use is a problem for him or her? Has the person been trying to cut back?

- What substances does the person use and how often? What are the effects on the person's ability to function?

- Are any of the following invitations to use for the person: being around drugs or alcohol, having extra money, or feeling frustrated?

- What time of day does the person use substances?

- What kinds of supports seem to help the person with abstinence or reduced use? (Be sure to listen carefully to the client here. Your assumptions about what *should* help may not be correct.)

Sometimes people are reluctant to talk about their substance use because they are ashamed, feel guilty, or have been lectured to in the past and want to avoid going through that again. Whatever the reason, it can be difficult to get accurate information about the person's substance use. Try to take a matter-of-fact, nonjudgmental attitude when you talk about this subject. Ask clients when they first started to use alcohol and how often and how much they drink currently. Follow the same approach with other drug use. Explain that your purpose in asking is to help with the person's employment goal and that you want to help the person plan so that substances won't affect a job. Be patient. Some people will become comfortable sharing information about substance use only after they have gotten to know you and trust that you will not judge or punish them.

You will also want to talk to others about the person's substance use pattern and history. Case managers, substance abuse counselors, and psychiatrists can all contribute information. Family members may have valuable information, as well. Talk to individuals about whether or not they want to include family members in discussions about substance use.

Duplicating this page is illegal. Do not copy this material without written permission from the publisher.

129

Example:

PLANNING FOR SOBRIETY ON THE JOB

Tim was a man in his late forties who wanted to work. He drank about a six-pack of beer every evening and usually got up about 11:00 in the morning. Tim knew that beer was bad for his health, but he didn't have any intention of quitting. The team talked about the type of job that might be a good fit for Tim and decided that a late-afternoon job would be important so that Tim would be sober and alert. Tim agreed with the plan. The employment specialist helped him find an afternoon job while the mental health team continued to focus on treatment issues.

Whether or not a person continues to use, the goal is to develop a job plan that will increase the likelihood that the person is sober while at work.

Find Jobs That Support Recovery

Even if a person has been abstinent for years, it is important to avoid jobs where alcohol is served. Anyone with a past or present diagnosis of substance use disorder should avoid work in bars and restaurants that serve alcoholic drinks. Other jobs can also be risky. For instance, some construction sites or factories are environments with a high rate of substance use.

Individuals may know that certain types of workplaces present problems for them. For example, some people may report that they are more likely to use if they work alone. Others may have difficulty resisting the temptation to steal over-the-counter medications when working at a drug store or grocery.

So what do you do when someone absolutely wants to work at a job that doesn't support sobriety? Each case can be a little different. If, for example, someone who drinks daily wanted assistance finding work at a bar, the treatment team would explain why they wouldn't feel right about supporting that goal. The employment specialist would not advocate with an employer in this situation, but would continue meeting with the person to discuss challenges and successes in his or her work life. The specialist might also continue to suggest other types of jobs. On the other hand, if someone with a background in construction work really wanted to find another drywalling job, the team could help with that goal while offering supports for substance abuse issues.

There is one more circumstance in which the team would not agree to help a person with a particular employment goal—when the goal might jeopardize the client's or someone else's safety. For instance, if a person smokes marijuana throughout the day, you wouldn't help that person find a roofing job. Sometimes safety becomes a concern after a client already has a job. It's important to consider what you would do if someone was working in a job and you believed the situation changed, and the person now was jeopardizing the safety of others. For example, suppose someone who had been sober had a relapse, and the team had reason to believe she might go to her bus-driving job even if she wasn't sober. In this situation, we recommend that the employment specialist and mental health practitioner speak to the mental health supervisor and/or psychiatrist immediately to determine the action necessary to ensure public safety. The steps taken by the team are then documented in the client's record.

Some employers use drug testing as part of the hiring process. Sometimes people manage to pass those tests in spite of ongoing substance use, and sometimes they don't. When clients fail drug tests, members of the mental health team talk to them to help them identify how their drug use is interfering with their goals, such as employment. However, the employment specialist also continues to help these clients look for other jobs that would support sobriety. Sometimes people manage to reduce or eliminate substance use long enough to pass drug tests. For example, people usually only need to abstain from cocaine or narcotics use for about a day to have a clean test, but regular, heavy users of marijuana may have positive test results for weeks. The team may hope that clients who use drugs will continue to reduce their use after finding work, but cutting down for a while can also be seen as a success.

Example of talking to clients about drug tests:

Albert:

I spoke to the manager who interviewed you, and he said that the reason you didn't get hired was because you failed the drug screening.

John:

I know I really should stop using.

Albert:

That's one possible solution. (Avoiding advice)

John:

Or, I could go to the health food store and get some of that stuff to clean my system out.

Albert:

I don't know much about that—whether or not those products are effective. But you're right that not everyone stops using drugs in order to get hired. Some people do and other people keep applying for jobs until they find an employer who doesn't drug-test. Others stay away from drugs during the job search, or at least prior to job interviews, because they know that a drug test might follow a positive job interview. (Avoiding advice)

John:

I could do that. If I know that I have an interview coming up, I'll stay away from using crack until I know whether or not the employer does drug tests.

Albert:

So, if your plan is to abstain just long enough to pass the drug test, then we should probably think about strategies that will help you to get to work sober. For instance, is there a particular time of day that you usually use drugs?

Most employment specialists report that they do not offer information about clients' substance use to employers simply because employers would almost certainly decline to hire. Instead, they help clients make job plans so that it is a reasonable assumption that the person will go to work sober. So, how can you handle it if an employer asks a direct question about a client's substance use? We never advise employment specialists to lie, but in many situations employment specialists will not have permission from the client to answer this question and will have to explain that they only have permission to share a limited amount of information. Employment specialists could also encourage the employer to ask the client directly.

Help Working People Manage Money

Money is a common trigger for substance use, particularly for people in the early stages of recovery. For instance, if a client doesn't yet believe that drugs are a problem in his or her life, that person is more likely to use extra income for drugs. However, if someone has been sober and actively involved in treatment for several months, he or she may be in a better position to handle extra income. Therefore, a plan to manage money should take the person's stage of recovery and personal history with money into account.

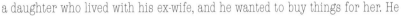

Examples of

MONEY MANAGEMENT PLANS:

Herb had been sober for six months when he became employed. He attended treatment groups on a regular basis and believed that his life would improve if he could remain sober. While Herb was looking for a job, the team talked to him about how he might handle his paychecks. Herb came up with the idea of having his paychecks deposited into a bank that was in the next town over—a little difficult for him to get to. He said that he had been doing well and that if the money was difficult to get at, he would probably be able to fight off an impulse to use.

John used alcohol and/or drugs almost every evening. He didn't believe that substances had a negative impact on his life, and he had no plans to quit. A payee managed John's Social Security check because John was impulsive, and money was definitely an invitation for him to use. However, when it came to getting a job, John would not agree to let the payee manage his work check. After John started a new job, an employment specialist who had a very good relationship with John made plans to pick him up from work on payday and take him shopping. John had

a daughter who lived with his ex-wife, and he wanted to buy things for her. He planned ahead and spent most of his check during a short period of time in the store on something that made him proud to have money. On the way home, the employment specialist reminded John that he would need to be in good shape to work the next day, and John agreed to drink less than usual that night. After John was accustomed to the shopping trips, his case manager took over the responsibility of taking him shopping on paydays, so that the employment specialist could focus on employment duties.

Example of

TREATMENT TEAM SUPPORT:

Alton had a long history of using cocaine, but he had been abstinent for several months when he started working at a hardware store. After two months of successful work, the employment specialist got a message from Alton's employer that he had missed two days of work without calling in. The team decided to reach out immediately and discovered that Alton had relapsed to cocaine use, not because of the job but due to his cousins moving into his home and bringing cocaine. The team arranged for Alton to find other housing, to return to Narcotics Anonymous, and to take a week off from work. After a week, Alton felt safe and supported, and the employment specialist helped him return to work.

Some clients may be willing to receive help with most of their check if they can keep a little extra spending money on hand. Most people will want that extra income to go toward something that they feel is important. For instance, if a payee is helping with the paycheck, the client could develop a plan with the payee to save some money for new clothes, an iPod, or a better place to live. Think about each person's values and goals when developing a money management plan. Also, be prepared to be flexible. As people begin to recover, they may want to assume more responsibility for their money. The team must be ready to alter the plan, even if that means taking a calculated risk.

Ask the Treatment Team to Plan and Provide Supports

Remember, as an employment specialist, you are not responsible for counseling the person about substance use, as that is really outside the scope of your expertise and role. Instead, the mental health and substance abuse practitioners can focus on helping the client recover from substance use disorder while you help the person with work.

For example, if the team is concerned about increased opportunities for substance use, they might offer treatment groups or other supports. If the team has concerns about particular triggers, such as co-workers going out for a beer, they can support the work plan by role-playing with the client so the person will have a ready response for the situation. It's helpful for the employment specialist to know how these interventions are going, but the specialist shouldn't suggest things to the client that the team hasn't already discussed.

The team can also help with setbacks. For instance, if a person begins to have job problems related to substance use, the team can help with treatment options while the employment specialist offers to assist with the job.

Emphasize Strengths and Foster Hope

People who have both mental illness and substance use disorders often have experienced many setbacks in their lives. It's difficult for some people to stay hopeful or even to recognize their own strengths after a series of problems. But people will make healthier choices when they build on their strengths, so employment specialists help people to recognize their abilities.

Try to point out the person's accomplishments along the way. Look for small improvements or new efforts that the person is making. Be sure to compliment the person in a genuine way. Don't lose credibility with the person by making a big deal out of a small matter—just point out things that you think are a step forward.

Take setbacks in stride. Remember that clients will likely feel ashamed if they run into problems because of substance use. Help them identify the things they did well, if even for a short time. Help them learn from the experience, and remember that you can also learn from the experience. With the new information you're learning, you may be able to help with a better job match or better job supports the next time. It can be through apparent setbacks that a person decides to make real changes and decides to reduce substance use.

Finally, talk to the person about long-term goals, including career development goals. Help the person envision different possibilities. Just by bringing up these ideas, you are sharing your belief that the person can have more out of life.

• • •

TOOLS FOR HELPING PEOPLE WHO HAVE CO-OCCURRING DISORDERS:

- View a video of an employment specialist and mental health team helping a person who has a co-occurring disorder. Go to www.dartmouth.edu/~ips/. Select "Resources," and then select "Videos." Choose the link "IPS Supported Employment Strategies That Work" and then select "Co-Occurring Disorders and Epilogue."

 Share information with other practitioners about helping people who have co-occurring disorders. For example, use the Information Sheet: Employment Supports for Clients with Co-occurring Mental Illness and Substance Use Disorders.

CHAPTER 9

Working on a Mental Health Team

The term *mental health treatment team* usually refers to a group of practitioners with various backgrounds of training and expertise. For example, a team could consist of case managers, therapists, nurses, employment specialists, a psychiatrist, and a housing expert. The idea is to gather together most of the people who work with the same group of clients so that they can share information and coordinate care. Teams meet at least once each week. The person most likely to run the weekly mental health team meeting is the mental health supervisor, though the IPS supervisor may visit team meetings regularly to talk about particular clients or to gauge how employment is integrated into the team. This is not an administrative meeting, but rather a meeting to review client situations and develop strengths-based strategies to promote recovery. The majority of meeting time is spent talking about clients.

The size of the mental health treatment team may also affect how well the team is able to function. If the team consists of practitioners who serve an aggregate caseload above 150 people, it becomes difficult to discuss all clients on a regular basis. People who are not experiencing crisis often fall to the side, and that might prevent the team from thinking about work or other goals for those people. Mental health treatments teams that serve 100–150 clients seem to be able to function well, provided that they have enough practitioners.

Mental health treatment team meetings as described here are different from individual planning meetings that occur less frequently (for example, one to four times per year) for updating service plans. Individual planning meetings include only the practitioners who directly provide services for the client. The client participates in the meetings and decides whether to invite family members and friends.

Mental health treatment teams ensure that services are integrated for clients, but they also provide an opportunity for practitioners to learn from each other. For example, employment specialists can learn more about mental illness and treatment during the meetings. Further, case managers and therapists have the opportunity to learn about jobs, accredited training programs, and education programs in the area. If a vocational rehabilitation

(VR) counselor attends the team meeting, that person can provide accurate information about VR services and the local job market.

Integration of services works best when practitioners know each other well. Therefore, it is optimal for each employment specialist to work with just one mental health team, though in some cases specialists may be involved with two teams. Employment specialists attend team meetings on a weekly basis. So, specialists who are attached to two teams will attend two mental health team meetings each week. Further, mental health practitioners and employment specialists talk between meetings to share information as it happens. It helps if their offices are close together or shared.

Finally, the team structure can help build an agency culture that supports work. Employment specialists can suggest work for clients who are discussed during team meetings. Sharing successes during team meetings also reinforces that people with mental illnesses, even those with psychotic symptoms or substance use disorders, can succeed at work.

Characteristics of a Successful Team

Though teams vary, three common characteristics help them succeed:

1. Shared decision-making

2. Clear practitioner roles

3. Regular involvement of medication prescribers

Shared Decision-Making

While brainstorming and developing plans, the team uses *shared decision-making*. This means that neither the case manager nor the employment specialist has the final call when it comes to the vocational plan. Rather, they each share their observations and attempt to come to an agreement regarding some options for a particular person. Ultimately, ideas from the team meeting will be taken to clients for their consideration.

The mental health treatment team meetings focus on planning, solving problems, and sharing successes. This means that all members participate throughout the entire team meeting. Rather than asking the employment specialist to provide updates at the beginning or end of the meeting, the employment specialist participates throughout the meeting like every other team member. The employment specialist may talk about clients who are having difficulties meeting goals or may choose to bring up someone who has just reached a new milestone at work.

Example of a mental health treatment team meeting:

Employment specialist:

I want to share the good news that Jane got offered a job yesterday and she is to begin work on Tuesday morning. She's going to be working at the quilt shop downtown, and she's really excited that she got hired because of her sewing skills.

Case manager:

That's great. How many hours will she work each week?

Employment specialist:

She's going to start with fifteen hours each week, but they'll ask her to work extra hours when they have sales. It will be a balancing act because of her benefits, but I think her boss will be flexible.

Psychiatrist:

I think the job sounds great, though Jane reports she is pretty groggy in the morning. Do you think that might be a problem?

Employment specialist:

The shop doesn't open until 10:00, so that helps. But I am a little concerned, particularly around the first week or two. I was planning to take Jane to work on Tuesday and Wednesday, but was hoping that someone could help me out on Friday.

Case manager:

Sure. I can do that.

Psychiatrist:

I might also want to suggest to Jane that she try taking her medication a little earlier than usual. That might help with the grogginess. But let me know if it starts to interfere with the job.

Team leader:

Well, that's great news. Let us know if it starts to look as though you'll need help with taking Jane to work next week.

As the example above illustrates, team meetings are a chance for everyone to share information and ideas. If a particular team member disagreed with the plan, the team meeting would be the place to voice concerns. However, the team would ultimately have to find a plan that all would support. Remember that one purpose of team meetings is to provide services in an integrated manner. If you feel strongly that the team plan will not be beneficial to the client, you should also talk to your supervisor.

Clear Practitioner Roles

Each person on the team has a specific role. The employment specialist, case manager, substance use counselor, psychiatrist, or others may all offer to help with an issue, but they all provide help within the scope of their positions.

Example of maintaining roles on a mental health treatment team:

Residential specialist:

I want to bring up Al. I smelled alcohol on his breath this weekend, but I didn't say anything. I wasn't sure how to bring it up.

Case manager:

He's been having such a hard time since his mom died. It may be that he's had a relapse.

Addiction counselor:

He missed my group last week, and that's not like Al.

Employment specialist:

I haven't spoken with Al's boss for a few weeks, but I'll give her a call this afternoon just to ask how things are going in general.

Case manager:

I'll try to catch Al this afternoon after his work shift to ask him if he's been drinking. His job is so important to him. If he is drinking, the possible loss of his job might be a great motivator for him to think about his alcohol use. Maybe Lou [employment specialist] and I can meet with Al together at some point. Let me know what you hear from Al's employer.

Addiction counselor:

After you talk to Al, let me know what he thinks about the group. I'd be glad to give him a phone call to remind him that it's okay to come back if he's slipped up.

There are times when team members may ask for help from one another. But, some roles on the team need to be protected. If, for example, employment specialists are asked to help with issues such as housing or transportation to medical appointments, they will likely lose their focus on employment and, as a result, the number of clients who find jobs will drop. But, as a member of the team, an employment specialist might help out on some occasions, for example, delivering medications when scheduled to meet with a client about job issues. Role protection for employment specialists applies even to Assertive Community Treatment (ACT) teams. Just as the psychiatrist doesn't take people grocery shopping, the employment specialist should not dilute his or her duties with case management activities.

Regular Involvement of Medication Prescribers
Psychiatrists and nurse practitioners should attend the weekly mental health treatment team meetings. Many clients report that a medication adjustment can be a very helpful job support. Further, medication prescribers can encourage clients to think about the possibility of going back to work and can reinforce the positive steps clients are taking toward achieving a working life.

If, however, the medication prescribers in your agency aren't able to attend weekly meetings, it is important to find other ways to communicate with them about the vocational plan. Below are some ideas for sharing information with medication prescribers:

- ☐ Ask if you can attend a staffing to discuss clients.
- ☐ Stop by the prescriber's office from time to time when you notice an open door. Don't take too much time, but share key bits of information about clients.
- ☐ Make sure that medication prescribers have your name and phone extension. Write it down for them and encourage them to call if they have questions or concerns.
- ☐ Use email, if available. Remember not to write long and involved emails. Medication prescribers usually have very tight schedules. Try to get to the point quickly.
- ☐ If possible, attend an occasional appointment with a client and the medication prescriber. This may be especially helpful if the person is having problems with symptoms or medication side effects on the job.

SUMMARY

The employment specialist is part of a mental health treatment team and reinforces the benefits of employment for clients served by that team. The employment specialist participates in team meetings and communicates regularly with team members outside of the meetings in order to provide coordinated, timely services.

Working on a mental health treatment team can provide learning opportunities for everyone on the team and can help foster an agency culture that supports work. Finally, the team can provide support to each other. Using the team format means that none of the practitioners has to work alone.

The Extended IPS Supported Employment Team

CHAPTER 10

Vocational Rehabilitation

In the United States, each state as well as the District of Columbia and U.S. territories supports a division of vocational rehabilitation (VR) offices throughout the state to provide vocational rehabilitation services for individuals with disabilities. Rehabilitation counselors at these offices sometimes provide direct services to clients and other times work with local programs (such as IPS supported employment programs) to provide assistance with employment. The focus of VR is to help people find gainful employment.

Eligibility for VR is determined on a client-by-client basis using three criteria established by federal law. To be eligible for VR services, a person must (1) have a physical, mental, or sensory impairment that constitutes or results in a substantial impediment to employment; (2) be able to benefit from VR services in terms of an employment outcome, though it is presumed that clients can benefit unless assessments suggest otherwise; and (3) require substantial VR services to prepare for, secure, retain, or regain employment. Further, if VR funds become strained at any point, many states use an "order of selection" to determine which eligible clients will be served first. Order of selection varies from state to state.

Rehabilitation counselors at VR can help clients think about an employment plan and can also help with a wide range of services, including job development, job coaching, and follow-along services. In some cases, VR is able to assist clients with job training, education programs, and the purchase of work uniforms, tools, or other items needed for work. Services must be related to the employment plan and vary from person to person.

To find your state office of Vocational Rehabilitation, go to http://askjan.org. Select "Job Seekers." Scroll down to "Federal, State, and Local Resources." Scroll down to "Vocational Rehabilitation Agencies (VR)."

Vocational rehabilitation counselors and IPS supported employment services can complement each other. In many cases, state VR counselors work side by side with IPS services. For example, VR counselors help develop the employment plan and may provide job leads or assist with various job supports.

IPS teams benefit from involvement with their local VR offices. VR counselors are knowledgeable about the local business community and can provide information about employers. Some clients have more than one disability, and VR counselors are knowledgeable about chronic physical illnesses and disabilities. Further, VR counselors often know many of the clients in the IPS program and are familiar with their past efforts to find and keep jobs.

In our work around the country, we've had contact with many VR counselors who report that IPS supported employment programs have helped to improve outcomes for people with severe and persistent mental illness. Although some of the concepts of IPS were new in the beginning (for example, ongoing work-based assessment rather than vocational evaluation or situational assessment), VR counselors reported that the extra help and individualized services provided by IPS supported employment seemed to make a difference.

VR and IPS Supported Employment Principles and Strategies

Many VR counselors have been inspired to become active participants in IPS and have asked for more information about the role of VR in IPS supported employment programs. This chapter outlines some of the strategies for providing services that are consistent with the principles of IPS. These strategies include

1 Integrated VR and IPS services

2 Zero exclusion

3 Respect for client preferences

4 Goal of competitive employment

5 Rapid job search

6 Benefits planning

7 Continuous job supports

Many of these strategies were developed by professionals working in the field. We recommend that practitioners from VR offices and IPS supported employment programs discuss these ideas and work together on new approaches in their own area.

The leaders of both VR and IPS programs can facilitate these strategies in several ways: They can meet to develop a shared philosophy grounded in evidence-based practices. They can remove barriers to collaboration, such as rules that might limit the development of teamwork between the two groups. Finally, they can focus on shared outcomes and training opportunities that help unite team members across programs.

Integrated VR and IPS Services

A number of years ago, *integrated services* referred to collaboration between the IPS team and mental health practitioners. More recently, however, we've been struck by the value of including VR counselors in the mental health treatment team. Doing so helps clients to hear consistent messages from everyone involved in their services. It also helps practitioners to sit down together and plan for ways to share talents and resources to benefit individual clients.

Participation in Team Meetings

Some programs invite vocational rehabilitation counselors to mental health treatment team meetings. These meetings consist of a multidisciplinary group of practitioners from the mental health center who gather to discuss individual clients and their goals. For instance, a treatment team meeting could include case managers, substance abuse counselors, nurses, employment specialists, housing staff, medication prescribers, and others. As each client is discussed, team members share information and suggest ways to help the person reach his or her goals. Attending these meetings can help vocational rehabilitation counselors learn more about what is happening in the person's treatment and the person's life. It's also a great way for vocational rehabilitation counselors to stay up-to-date on medication and treatment for mental illness. In return, vocational rehabilitation counselors can contribute their own unique perspective and increase the team's awareness of the importance of work for persons with disabilities. Inviting a person from outside the mental health center to attend team meetings may be a new challenge for the agency. At first there are often concerns about confidentiality. Program administrators should meet to develop strategies to allow rehabilitation counselors to attend treatment team meetings as full-fledged members (please see the end of this chapter, page 156).

Monthly Meetings

Another strategy for integrated services is monthly meetings between the VR counselor(s) and the IPS unit. Often, the monthly meetings are used to quickly review shared cases. Extra time is reserved to talk about individuals who are having difficulty meeting their employment goals. In addition, time is spent discussing potential referrals from the IPS unit. These meetings are most effective if both the VR and IPS supervisors attend.

Co-location of VR and IPS

Co-location appears to be one of the most effective strategies for building inter-agency collaboration. In this model, a VR counselor has office space at the mental health center. The counselor is usually present two to three days each month and shares the space with other part-time staff. As mental health practitioners become aware of the days that the VR counselor is on site, they often make a point of stopping by to ask questions, share information, and bring in clients. In fact, rehabilitation counselors report that seeing clients at the mental health center is a great way to reduce their "no-show" rate. Programs report that one of the best unintended consequences of co-location is greatly improved relationships between mental health practitioners and VR counselors. As people from both programs eat lunch together, celebrate birthdays, and develop personal relationships, coordination of services begins to flow naturally. For co-location to be effective, rehabilitation counselors need to have access to the Internet, privacy for interviewing clients, access to a copier, and so on. We recommend that mental health agency administrators meet with VR supervisors to discuss issues such as resource needs and confidentiality prior to making arrangements for co-location.

Assigned VR Liaisons

Assignment of one or two VR liaisons to the IPS supported employment program may do much to improve integration. Because rehabilitation counselors have high caseloads, they may not be able to sit in extra meetings or to spend extra time at the mental health center unless a significant proportion of their caseload is participating in IPS. Therefore, IPS supported employment referrals are sometimes routed to just one or two rehabilitation counselors, rather than to all the counselors in the office. VR supervisors who use this approach usually think about the counselors in their office who have expressed interest in working with people who have severe mental illnesses.

Zero Exclusion

While IPS programs work with people for extended periods of time even when their progress is slow, rehabilitation counselors need to demonstrate that clients are making steady progress toward their goals in order to keep their cases open,

■ ■ ■

June Stewart is a VR counselor who is integrated with a mental health program in Minnesota. Here are her thoughts about this approach to providing services:

I receive all of the referrals from the mental health team, and I spend part of my week right there in their office. The desk I use is in the same area as everyone else. I also participate in the team meetings once a week. What I try to do in that time is bring an employment viewpoint to the discussion and give hints about what people could do to get started with work. It's very useful to me, as well, to hear information about my clients. For example, one person said she really wanted to work, but then I couldn't reach her. At a team meeting I heard that she's had some medical issues. In the past I would have closed the case, but once I understood why she wasn't available, I kept it open.

I stay in close contact with the employment specialist. We have contact several times each week to bounce ideas off each other, and we also see each other in the treatment team meetings. I think that we each have helpful information to share with each other.

It does take time to be integrated into the team, but in the past it was hard to catch up with case managers on the phone since they were in the field a lot. I was also frustrated at times because mental health practitioners don't always stay in their jobs for long, so I was constantly retraining mental health workers about vocational things. This way, it is easy to be face-to-face with them to talk about what I do or to bring the work perspective to things.

The integrated services work because I know the team members and they know me. There is a level of trust. We feel free to ask questions of each other, and there is a lot of respect for each other's knowledge. It's a wonderful team.

and most cases are not open for long periods of time. Therefore, IPS programs refer *most* clients to VR, rather than all. Sometimes VR counselors and IPS programs decide that some people will receive services only from the IPS teams. For example, if a person wanted to begin by working just two hours per week, and slowly add more work hours, that client might not be a good referral to VR until he or she was ready to work more hours. Or, if a person felt ambivalent about returning to work and, therefore, was missing many appointments, the mental health team and IPS unit might work with the client until his or her interest in work increased and then make a referral to VR. Of course, none of us has a crystal ball. The person we think will need extra time to build a working life may very well exceed everyone's expectations. Therefore, even if a person is not initially referred to vocational rehabilitation, the IPS unit should provide the best employment services possible and make the referral when the individual demonstrates progress.

That being said, we encourage rehabilitation counselors to think about eligibility in a new way. Traditional vocational evaluation and performance in sheltered work settings are not good predictors of vocational success for people with mental illnesses. In fact, clients often become frustrated and embarrassed by these remedial steps and then drop out of services. Instead of using traditional methods to determine eligibility, we suggest that counselors use information from the mental health center related to the person's interest in work, the person's supports for going back to work, and any other information that the employment specialist has gathered in advance of the VR appointment. For example, at one IPS program, the employment specialist usually begins meeting with clients a few weeks before their VR appointment. The employment specialist begins the career profile and, by the VR intake appointment, has detailed information about the person's goals, life situation, and treatment issues.

Historically, many rehabilitation counselors have screened people from services based on issues such as substance use or significant psychotic symptoms. However, research has demonstrated that such problems do not accurately predict whether or not a particular individual will be successful at work. We urge you to consider working with some people whom you may not have made eligible for services in the past. If, as a VR counselor, you feel uncomfortable with this suggestion, ask to sit down with the IPS supervisor and review the IPS program outcomes. You may find that you are missing out on some successful closures. Talk to the supervisor about how to increase shared cases and shared outcomes. Also, please consider reading chapter 8, which focuses on people with co-occurring disorders.

Respect for Client Preferences

Vocational rehabilitation values helping people with goals that are consistent with their lifestyle, personality, and preferences. IPS supported employment shares this philosophy and also places a high value on client preferences. Job preferences may include job location, work schedule, type of work, disclosure of disability, type of job environment, and other factors. Though this level of specificity can make job finding a little more difficult, a very good job fit can help mitigate some of the effects of severe mental illnesses.

The work shift is one preference to which IPS programs pay particular attention. Some people with severe mental illnesses may not have worked in many years or may not be able to tolerate the stress of a forty-hour or even twenty-hour work week. Particularly in the beginning, some clients report that they need to start slow and gradually build their work hours.

In some states, mental health programs are able to work independently with people who want to start with very limited hours. In others, rehabilitation counselors make an effort to open cases for some people who need limited hours. These cases are balanced by the majority of people with mental illnesses who want to work twenty hours or more. Rehabilitation counselors recognize that some people who start work with very limited hours will eventually increase the amount that they work.

Goal of Competitive Employment

Just like vocational rehabilitation, IPS supported employment programs focus on regular jobs in the community. IPS helps people find permanent positions that pay at least minimum wage. The definition of *competitive work* used for this evidence-based practice is as follows:

- Workers are paid at least minimum wage. If others in similar positions earn more than minimum wage, the IPS client would earn the same rate.

- Workers are paid directly by their employer. Wages are not filtered through a mental health agency or vocational vendor.

- These jobs are not set aside for workers with disabilities. Having a disability is not a requirement to be hired for one of these jobs. An exception may be a *peer specialist position* in which experience living with mental illness is a requirement for the job.

- In addition, job tenure is not negotiated by a vocational vendor or mental health agency. For example, transitional employment positions are not considered to be competitive jobs.

IPS supported employment programs do not focus on jobs that are based in enclaves, even if the pay is above minimum wage. Instead, IPS looks to find positions that are open to anyone regardless of a disability in order to promote inclusion and reduce stigma.

In some states, sheltered workshops are becoming less segregated. For example, the workshops may hire people from the community who don't have disabilities as well as people with disabilities, and the pay is often above minimum wage. Many times, clients accept these jobs because they are readily available, even though they may not match their preferences. Other clients may take these jobs because they have been receiving mental health services for so long that they've become accustomed to "living in the system" and have stopped hoping to achieve the things they wanted before they became ill. But just like vocational rehabilitation, IPS supported employment programs want to help people become active members of the community who live and work alongside everyone else.

Rapid Job Search

In IPS supported employment, *rapid job search* refers to making contact with employers within a few weeks of the first appointment with an employment specialist. Rather than spend time on evaluation, situational assessment, or work adjustment, programs help clients begin the job search right away. Research has demonstrated that for people with mental illnesses, a rapid job search leads to better employment outcomes.

Think about some of the clients you've known and how they adjusted to jobs. You may be able to remember a person who did terribly in one work environment and just fine in another, even though the job tasks were very similar. Vocational evaluations and situational assessments just can't provide the critical information that you need to determine which job will be a good fit. The variables involved with each job are simply too great. For example, when people go out in the work world, they may encounter a very supportive boss or a critical boss. Someone may be highly motivated to keep a job that is within walking distance of his or her home. Because employers are sometimes willing to make accommodations and because clients sometimes have increased motivation to perform well at regular jobs, the limited information provided by evaluations does not predict success in the real world.

Therefore, IPS supported employment programs help people think about their work needs and strengths by gathering information about functioning, personal values, preferences, symptoms, medication side effects, and previous work history.

Important information may be found in the person's clinical record and work history. Further, the work candidate, mental health clinicians, and family members have information to share.

■ ■ ■

Below, Claire Beck, Assistant District Supervisor, Division of Vocational Rehabilitation in Missouri, describes how she made the transition to a rapid job search:

I've been a mental health counselor with VR for seventeen years, and one source of my referrals is our state hospital. These people are incarcerated because of forensic issues and they are usually people who have a lot of barriers to employment. After I attended a state meeting about IPS supported employment, I received three new referrals from the state hospital. I thought I would try an experiment with rapid job search. Each person wanted to work and had a job goal, so I suggested that we just try job development and skip the assessment. I was surprised that two of the three people found jobs within a few months. The third person got job offers but turned them down due to his psychosis.

Until a couple of years ago, we used evaluations routinely, but since that experiment, I've continued to use the rapid job search approach for almost everyone. I find that people are happier with the service. In the past, people complained about assessments because they didn't see how that was getting them a job. Rapid job search works well for me and for my clients.

Just like everyone else, clients can find out what works for them by trying a real job. Many people are successful at the first job because of the time they spent thinking about jobs with their VR counselor, employment specialist, and treatment team. But when a job doesn't work out, the person and service providers take time to think about what can be learned from the job experience. Then, using those lessons, they encourage the person to find another job that is a better match. This means that some clients need to try more than one job to be successful.

However, if you think about the people you have served over the years, you may recall that many people needed to try more than one job, whether or not the disability was mental illness.

In order to help people with a rapid job search, many VR offices have tried to expedite eligibility and placement authorizations. To help with this, the mental health agencies work hard to ensure that the rehabilitation counselor has the needed reports with proper signatures at the time of referral. In some cases, rehabilitation counselors are able to quickly find clients eligible, write a plan, and authorize job placement—sometimes within an appointment or two. In other cases, the VR counselor must first find information related to secondary disabilities or help people with health care issues. In these situations, the mental health staff may assist clients with appointments or releases of information.

As a VR counselor, you help the employment specialist with job search activities. Because you work with so many people, you have a bird's-eye view of the employer community. You may be aware of employers and jobs that the employment specialist doesn't know about. You can help by sharing ideas for job leads on a regular basis.

Further, you can encourage employment specialists to get out into the community to meet with employers. We think you'll find that the programs that get the most jobs are those in which staff spends a lot of time meeting employers. We encourage employment specialists to carve out time to make contacts with employers every week. Because you're a funder of job development services, your support for this approach can go a long way.

Benefits Planning

Every person who receives benefits should get accurate information about the impact of earned income on entitlements. Information should be provided not just about Social Security work incentives, but also on housing subsidies, food stamps, benefits received by spouses and children, and so on. Every source of income should be considered.

We recommend that benefits planning be provided by a person who has received extensive training and who continues to stay up-to-date on new information regarding benefits. Further, we encourage service providers to ask for written reports that include individualized information about the impact of wages on benefits.

In some areas, mental health centers offer benefits planning through an employment specialist who is trained and specializes in benefits. Some states have systems of benefits planners available. Regardless of the options for benefits information, rehabilitation counselors can help by advocating for accurate benefits planning if it appears that clients are not receiving good information.

Continuous Job Supports

Initially, a combination of vocational rehabilitation and mental health supports is optimal. However, IPS programs have more flexibility to provide supports over the long term. The continuous job supports provided by IPS supported employment programs are attractive to many rehabilitation counselors who have seen clients struggle with job retention over the years. Although rehabilitation counselors must close cases after jobs appear to be stable, IPS programs work alongside case managers and other treatment providers to ensure that job supports are available to clients as they need them.

VR and Mental Health Leadership: Engendering a Shared Philosophy

Before asking practitioners to embark on collaboration to provide IPS supported employment services, VR and mental health leaders should meet to discuss the evidence-based practice. If leaders determine that IPS is in keeping with each program's mission, then supervisors should not only take steps to implement change, but should also express their support for the new practice. Change is difficult for all people, but leaders can help staff embrace new ideas by talking about the goals of change, asking practitioners for ideas about how to make changes, and sharing their excitement about helping people with mental illness to move ahead with recovery. Here are some of the underpinnings of IPS:

- People with severe mental illnesses have strengths, talents, abilities, and experiences that they can bring to the workforce. Practitioners are encouraged to be hopeful and respectful.

- Individualized services help people with mental illnesses to find and keep jobs. Practitioners are valued for their efforts to be creative problem solvers.

- IPS supported employment works best if the resources and talents of multiple systems are shared. Practitioners are supported as they practice shared decision-making. They are encouraged to learn from each other.

- Research can help mental health and VR think about strategies to adjust service provision and improve outcomes. Practitioners are esteemed for their interest in learning.

Removal of Barriers to Collaboration

Leaders should meet to talk about the current service system and barriers to IPS implementation. For example, as mentioned above, improving integration between mental health and VR might mean developing strategies to include rehabilitation counselors as treatment team members while still observing confidentiality policies. Another example is the quote from the VR counselor June Stewart, who talked about how her job had changed since she began working closely with the team (see page 149). She mentioned that the time needed for integration had been built into her job so she could work closely with the treatment team.

There may also be informal barriers to practicing IPS. For example, although state VR systems may not have a written policy against writing more than one job placement authorization for an individual, some offices may have developed practices that do not support second or third placements. In this case, supervisors and administrators would need to work together to determine how each system can best support clients who need to try more than one job.

Shared Outcomes

Improved outcomes are a primary reason that people from various systems want to work together. Careful monitoring of outcomes will help maintain motivation to improve collaboration. IPS supervisors and vocational rehabilitation supervisors can meet quarterly to discuss current outcomes and devise strategies to improve future outcomes. IPS supervisors and vocational rehabilitation supervisors may even decide to set common goals. For example, they may set a goal for the number of people who will find jobs during the coming year, as well as the number of people who will keep jobs for at least ninety days. These outcomes are important to both programs.

Shared Training Opportunities

Being part of the IPS supported employment team means that rehabilitation counselors must be knowledgeable about IPS. As much as possible, VR counselor liaisons and supervisors should participate in initial and ongoing workshops about IPS supported employment. Other training that focuses on key components of IPS (for example, motivational interviewing and job development) should also be supported.

Ideally, supervisors, employment specialists, and rehabilitation counselors will attend training together so that they can talk about new ideas in the moment. Leadership from both systems can co-sponsor training opportunities, help practitioners develop performance goals that include training, and provide access to written material such as journal articles or books.

• • •

TOOLS TO IMPROVE COLLABORATION BETWEEN VOCATIONAL REHABILITATION AND IPS SUPPORTED EMPLOYMENT PROGRAMS:

Strategies for Collaboration between IPS Supported Employment Programs and State Vocational Rehabilitation: Use this handout to start a discussion about strategies for collaboration.

- IPS supported employment newsletter (Winter 2010). Focus on Vocational Rehabilitation. Go to http://www.dartmouth.edu/~ips. Select "Free Newsletter." Select "Previous Newsletters," then "Winter 2010."

Supervision of IPS Supported Employment

Please note: This chapter focuses on the role of IPS supervisors. However, other people (such as clinical supervisors, agency administrators, and clients) should also read this chapter to learn about effective practices for IPS supervisors.

The most important function of an IPS supervisor is to ensure that the program has good outcomes. The purpose of an IPS program is to help people with their employment and education goals. It's that simple. Therefore, a program is not judged by its number of employment specialists or the amount of revenue generated by the program. Rather, the program is a success if most people who enter the program are able to find and keep jobs that meet their preferences.

Over the years, we've observed that programs with good outcomes almost always have strong supervisors. Most employment specialists are new to IPS supported employment when they are hired and rely on the supervisor to teach them their jobs. Further, teams usually look to the supervisor to set the tone of the workplace. For instance, if a supervisor always talks about clients in a hopeful and positive manner, the team is likely to mimic that behavior. Supervisors are in a position to affect every element of IPS services. Good supervision is critical to IPS program success.

Strategies to Achieve and Sustain Good Outcomes

In this chapter, we'll discuss strategies that IPS supervisors can use to improve and sustain good outcomes. We believe that supervisors must fulfill three basic roles:

1   Teacher

2   Quality assurance manager

3   Liaison

Let's explore each of these roles.

The IPS Supervisor as Teacher

It is unusual for supervisors of any type to view themselves as teachers. Most supervisors feel that their responsibility includes providing orientation for new employees as well as ongoing office-based supervision. However, since it's rare to hire employment specialists who have any IPS experience—most supervisors feel fortunate when they are able to hire someone with *any* related experience—IPS supervisors must be prepared to take on the role of teacher to ensure that employment specialists will provide high-quality services.

As a supervisor, you will spend some time in the office providing information about IPS supported employment and talking to practitioners about individual clients. Talking to people about how to provide services gives them a vision about how services should look. And helping employment specialists think of strategies to help individual clients is also important. But, neither activity is sufficient. That's because most people learn best by watching someone perform a skill and then trying it out themselves with help and immediate feedback. It isn't possible for supervisors to anticipate the obstacles that employment specialists will encounter when they are doing their jobs. Therefore, we strongly urge supervisors to get into the field with practitioners to help them learn needed skills.

Examples of supervisors working with employment specialists:

A new employment specialist attended training on job development and felt great about the strategies that she learned. But, as she was going out to meet her first employer, she stopped in the middle of the parking lot because she wasn't sure how to ask for the manager of the business. The supervisor explained how she usually asked for the hiring manager and offered to take the lead during that employer contact.

■ ■ ■

An employment specialist reported that one of her clients didn't want to work. When the supervisor went with the employment specialist to meet the person, he learned that the specialist had asked the client to meet in order to talk about good communication skills, rather than to job hunt. The client, who wanted a job, was very frustrated with this process. The employment specialist genuinely wanted to help her client—she just really believed that the person needed to improve her communication skills. When the client began missing appointments, she assumed that she didn't want to work. The supervisor assessed the situation and suggested that the specialist and client make plans to go job hunting the next day. Back in the office, the supervisor reinforced the rationale for rapid job search and helped the specialist think of jobs that didn't require great communication skills. The next day, the specialist went with her client to apply for two jobs and they were actually able to speak to one manager after turning in an application. The client felt great about speaking to the manager. The employment specialist continued to have some concerns about her client's communication skills, but the supervisor followed the situation closely to ensure that the job search continued to move forward.

In each of these situations, the supervisor needed to be in the field to assess what was really going on and also to provide help. Supervisors cannot be present all of the time, but by going out with staff periodically, they can demonstrate approaches to different situations. Further, the supervisor will have an accurate picture of the employment specialist's skills and areas for development.

Teaching Job Development
Supervisors can provide field mentoring for any aspect of the vocational process, including engagement, career profile, job development, job supports, and career development. Although we encourage supervisors to attend to all of these areas, we've observed that job development is a skill with which many employment specialists have difficulty.

Some supervisors resist going out with specialists to conduct employer contacts because they feel that other, experienced people on the team can mentor their peers. They send new employment specialists out to shadow their co-workers. Although this can be helpful, it is not sufficient. When supervisors go out, they can do more than shadow. To teach job development, supervisors can first model employer contacts, then observe the specialist conducting a contact, and finally discuss areas that the specialist handled well and strategies the specialist might try the next time.

Other supervisors resist job development because they themselves don't have experience in this area. However, by going out with all team members, supervisors will quickly learn about methods that work, as well as methods that are ineffective. If you are in this situation, explain to your team that you want to learn more about job development from them. Practitioners will appreciate your willingness to get involved and really try to understand what their jobs are like. Rather than losing credibility with your staff, you will likely gain their respect. Further, if you

Duplicating this page is illegal. Do not copy this material without written permission from the publisher.

161

go out frequently, you will soon begin to feel confident about job development and will then be able to help teach new employment specialists who are struggling with employer contacts.

Be sure to read chapter 5, "Helping People Find Employment." When scheduling job development with specialists, try to help with different phases of employer relationship building. For example, help them schedule appointments with employers, learn about employer business needs, talk about clients who are looking for jobs, and follow up with employers over time.

On the CD-ROM, you'll find logs for field mentoring, including one specific to job development. These logs can help you and a specialist plan carefully for each contact—one of the skills you will be trying to teach. The logs will also help you keep a record of supervision and will keep both of you on track with a plan to improve specific skills.

When you and the specialist go out to meet with employers, take the lead with the first employer. This will give the specialist a chance to observe your tone, manner, and the specific things you say. When you visit the next employer, ask the specialist to take the lead, and then take turns for the remaining employer visits. Share feedback with the specialist, but also ask the person to give you feedback after you conduct a visit. The idea is to learn from each other so that the specialist doesn't feel like he or she is under the microscope. Further, if you lead a contact that goes badly, use it as a learning experience to show that every contact will not be perfect. One supervisor shared the following story about field mentoring with a specialist. He said that when he took the lead with an employer, he couldn't get the employer to put down his newspaper to talk to him. In fact, he never even saw the employer's face. He and the specialist just laughed about it and went on to the next business.

When you hire a new employment specialist, remember that the person may be intimidated at the thought of marching into a business and speaking with an employer. Think about the level of support that you would appreciate if you were in that situation. Set up a plan to help the person learn job development.

SAMPLE PLAN FOR TEACHING JOB DEVELOPMENT

1. Ask the employment specialist to read chapter 5 of this manual. Meet with the specialist to review the chapter.

2. Watch a video demonstration with the specialist about job development. (See the tool box at the end of this chapter to find a job development video.) Discuss the videos together.

3. Set aside a few hours to go out with the specialist to conduct employer contacts. Before heading out, talk about the purpose of each contact and decide who will take the lead. Use the Field Mentoring Log for Job Development (see "tools" at the end of this chapter) to help lead you through this process. Be sure to take the lead with the first employer contact, and then take turns.

4. Plan to go out with the specialist to do job development weekly for the first month, and at least monthly for the first six months of the specialist's employment.

5. Arrange for the specialist to shadow other people on the team who have good employment outcomes.

6. Review at least a couple of job development logs with the specialist during each office-based supervision session. Ask the employment specialist to describe the purpose of the visit, the way that he or she prepared for the visit, reactions from the employer, and so on. Help the specialist make plans to follow up with the employer.

7. After the specialist has been employed for at least six months and demonstrates the ability to build relationships with employers, provide field mentoring on a quarterly basis. Even accomplished specialists can continue to learn about job development. Having a supervisor along for the ride encourages people to be more thoughtful about their approach and, consequently, leads to more learning. As a supervisor, you can also share effective strategies you have observed with other team members.

Helping the Team Learn about Job Supports

Providing individualized job supports is another area in which employment specialists typically need help. Although most practitioners feel confident about the job supports they provide, it is easy to underestimate the level of supports clients need, and difficult to provide individualized supports. The following strategies can help you teach individualized job supports to your team:

☐ Make a point of knowing as many people as possible who are served by your team. Go out with employment specialists as they are engaging clients and conducting career profiles so that you get to know the people on their caseload (the added benefit will be that you can demonstrate effective approaches to engagement, good client interviewing skills, and so on). Try to learn at least some basic information about the work history and mental health history of people served by the team. When clients become employed, you will be in a much better position to provide suggestions about needed job supports.

☐ Sit in meetings with employment specialists as they talk about job supports with clients. Listen to whether specialists offer the same assistance to everyone; for instance, holding weekly meetings and encouraging clients to call if they have problems. Make suggestions about other supports, such as wake-up calls for a person who has a new morning job.

☐ Attend mental health team meetings on the weeks that people get hired. Model how to involve mental health practitioners in discussions about job supports. For example, "Does anyone have any concerns about this job?" "What type of supports might be helpful?" "Would it make sense to contact the client's family about this new job to see if they can help with supports?"

☐ Use the weekly IPS supported employment meeting to help the entire group learn about job supports. Model good planning by working as a team to develop individualized supports for clients. For example, when someone is hired, ask the employment specialist to bring copies of the person's career profile to the meeting. Then ask the employment specialist to share information about the following four areas:

• **Work history:** Ask the employment specialist to describe the person's work history, including favorite jobs and reasons for job endings.

• **Strengths:** Ask for a description of the client's strengths, experiences, skills, and preferences.

- **Concerns:** Ask the specialist and others who may know the client to try to anticipate any difficulties that could arise with the new job related to symptoms, cognitive problems, substance use, transportation, and so on.
- **Supports:** Ask about family members and friends. (This is a good time to remind employment specialists that, with permission, they should include the person's supports in the employment plan.)

After the specialist has provided brief (three- or four-minute) descriptions on each topic, help the team brainstorm strategies to maximize the person's strengths and prevent anticipated problems. For example, if the person doesn't know why he or she lost jobs in the past, the team might conclude that the person doesn't pick up on feedback from employers. They would then anticipate that the person could have problems understanding feedback on this new job and design supports to help the person receive extra feedback. Or if a person is relying on her grandmother to pick her up from work at midnight three days a week, she might anticipate that her grandmother will not be able to provide transportation indefinitely. While brainstorming supports that will help clients avoid problems, include details such as frequency and location of services. Finally, ask the employment specialist to take the team's suggestions to clients for discussion. Ultimately, clients will choose the supports that they feel are best.

Teaching Client-Interviewing Skills
In chapter 3, we described effective ways to interact with clients. Interviewing skills included active listening (including the use of reflections), open-ended questions, expressing empathy, maintaining focus, avoiding advice, avoiding arguments, and closing the interview. Although these strategies sound relatively straightforward, it is actually quite difficult to learn these techniques and to integrate them into routine interactions with clients. The bottom line is that unless supervisors practice these skills with employment specialists, the employment specialists are not going to use the skills.

Supervisors can help by providing opportunities for employment specialists to think about the techniques, observe the techniques, practice the techniques, and receive feedback. Group supervision, individual supervision, and job shadowing can be occasions for specialists to learn and refine interviewing skills.

For example, during a team meeting, a supervisor might talk about reflections. Next, he or she would demonstrate reflections in a short role-play, asking one of the employment specialists to play a client while he or she takes the role of an employment specialist. Employment specialists could then break into pairs to role-play with each other, while the supervisor moves about the room listening and providing suggestions. Finally, the supervisor could ask each employment specialist to concentrate on using reflections during his or her interactions with clients during the week. As a follow-up, the supervisor would ask the specialists to report back on their experiences during the next IPS supported employment meeting.

During individual supervision, a supervisor could ask the employment specialist to practice a technique together. For instance, if an employment specialist expresses frustration about a client who will not dress up to apply for jobs, the supervisor may view that as an opportunity to practice avoiding arguments. The practice sessions will be most helpful if the supervisor first discusses the technique of avoiding arguments, then models the behavior by taking the role of the employment specialist, and finally requests that the employment specialist practice the behavior while the supervisor takes the role of the client.

Another very useful approach is to observe an employment specialist interacting with an actual client. The advantage to this approach is that the employment specialist is practicing the technique in the exact environment in which it is needed. Being observed may feel a little uncomfortable to employment specialists at first, but if the supervisor makes a habit of occasionally observing everyone on the team, that should lessen the discomfort. If the supervisor continues to use this approach over time, employment specialists will eventually view the observations as business as usual.

Directly after the client meeting, the supervisor and employment specialist can meet to talk about the techniques that the employment specialist used. The supervisor might start the discussion by asking the employment specialist for his or her impressions of the meeting. Then the supervisor might comment on strengths demonstrated by the specialist, as well as make some suggestions for improvement.

To learn more about interviewing techniques, supervisors and employment specialists may wish to attend training on motivational interviewing. Many practitioners try to attend at least one workshop on motivational interviewing each year. Finally, visit the Web site www.motivationalinterview.org.

Helping Specialists Access Information about Mental Illness
Some employment specialists will not have a background in mental health. In these situations, encourage the specialists to attend local workshops and in-services

that are related to mental health and mental health treatment. Going to the mental health treatment team meeting each week will also help specialists learn about mental illnesses. If it is possible for specialists to attend staffing with psychiatrists, it will be time well spent.

In addition, you can offer some simple reading material to new employment specialists and also review the material with them during individual supervision. For instance, basic information about mental illnesses can be found in the Illness Management and Recovery Evidence-Based Practices KIT (SMA09-4463). Go to www.samhsa.gov. Click on "Site Map" at the bottom of the page. Select "Publications." Go to "Issues, Conditions, & Disorders" at the top of the page, and then select "Mental Illness." The National Alliance on Mental Illness (NAMI) Web site includes information about mental illness: http://www.nami.org/Template.cfm?Section=By_Illness, as well as information about medications: http://www.nami.org/template.cfm?section=about_medications.

Group Supervision as a Teaching Tool
Group supervision (vocational unit meetings) is an effective method to develop staff skills and improve the quality of program services. Meetings are an opportunity to provide education and to work on specific team issues. The focus of the meetings is to talk about people served by the team, not to work on administrative issues such as documentation or productivity. Below is a sample agenda for an IPS supported employment unit meeting:

IPS Supported Employment Unit Meeting
March 20XX

I. Prep for CARF accreditation visit ▶	Pilar, IPS supervisor ▶	5 minutes
II. Update on VR order of selection ▶	Bob, VR counselor ▶	5 minutes
III. Celebrations ▶	All ▶	10 minutes
IV. Client discussions ▶	All ▶	20 minutes
V. Clients in job search 4 months or longer ▶	All ▶	15 minutes
VI. Review of assignments ▶	Pilar ▶	5 minutes

You'll note that a vocational rehabilitation counselor attended the IPS team meeting. As noted in chapter 10, more and more, IPS supported employment teams are finding benefits to working closely with their local vocational rehabilitation offices. They report that close collaboration results in better services for clients. To that end, many programs are inviting rehabilitation counselors to attend employment unit meetings once a month or more, as well as an occasional mental health treatment team meeting. Although rehabilitation counselors may not have the flexibility to attend every meeting, the team makes an effort to make them feel welcome.

Celebrations are an important part of IPS supported employment. Throughout this manual, we've stressed the importance of staying hopeful. One way to promote hope on your team is to share success stories. The successes can be striking, such as someone finding a job, or less obvious, such as someone finally meeting with the employment specialist. Some teams go around the room and ask each person to share one or two positive events from the previous week. Supervisors carefully respond to the stories in an encouraging manner.

Clients to be discussed during the meeting are often suggested by employment specialists, the vocational rehabilitation counselor (if present), and the IPS supported employment supervisor. A common practice is to ask team members to write client first names on a dry-erase board as they enter the room. This allows the supervisor to determine which clients need a longer discussion and helps him or her to keep the meeting organized and on schedule. In the agenda above, the supervisor asked the team to spend some time talking about people who had been job searching for more than four months. The team could talk about ideas to enhance the job search for those clients, ideas about businesses that are hiring, and so forth. In another meeting, the supervisor might ask the team to discuss job support plans or review clients who have been difficult to engage.

The tone of these meetings is always respectful toward the people served by the program. Sarcasm is not permitted. If an employment specialist is feeling frustrated, the team offers to help the specialist out rather than malign the client. For example, the team might brainstorm strategies to move the client's job search forward, and the supervisor might offer to go out with the specialist to meet with the person. Clients need to feel that their specialist is on their side. If the team is not focused on strengths and client goals, outcomes will suffer and the mission of the program (to help people achieve recovery through work) is severely compromised. A common problem that leads to frustration is when the employment specialist feels that someone doesn't really want to work. When this happens, consider going to the mental health treatment team with the specialist to talk about the situation. Work with the team to find out which obstacles are getting in the person's way, and whether or not the person is interested in employment in the immediate future. Also, try to find out if there is something the employment specialist could do differently in order to make the services more attractive to the person. For example, ask if the mental health practitioners heard the client's opinion about the IPS services. Does the client feel hopeful about finding a job that he or she will like? Does the client appear to feel comfortable with the employment specialist and have a good relationship?

Supervisors can even increase the level of commitment that specialists feel toward their jobs by reinforcing the program's mission during unit meetings. One supervisor we know occasionally makes statements like, "The work that we do breaks down stigma, one employer at a time. I live in this community and I don't want to live in a place where people have stigma about mental illness. You are making a difference."

Some supervisors report that weekly meetings are not necessary, as they have daily contact with employment specialists and are providing supervision throughout the day. However, unit meetings are not meant to take the place of "in-the-moment supervision." Rather, the meetings augment that supervision by providing opportunities for team members to take their time to think through issues and share ideas about how to help clients. Team meetings provide an opportunity to *plan* services rather than react to situations.

At the end of each meeting, the supervisor quickly reviews the outcome of each discussion and the follow-up steps team members have agreed to take. During the meeting, the supervisor takes notes about the issues and proposed solutions. At a later time, the supervisor will check back with the employment specialist to ask how he or she was able to implement the proposed solutions. These notes help the supervisor keep track of work that needs to get done, but they also serve as a record of supervision provided to the team. It is strongly recommended that IPS supported employment supervisors save supervision notes in a locked filing cabinet or in accordance with their agency's policies.

In addition to helping the team learn, weekly meetings are a great way to build a sense of teamwork. Employment specialists who spend much of their time on the road report that they appreciate the opportunity to connect with their peers and feel that they are not alone in their work.

Orientation for New Employment Specialists
To ensure that you introduce all the necessary subjects to each new specialist, we recommend using a checklist such as the sample checklist on page 170. You might give this checklist to each new specialist and then help the person make

plans to complete the activities. It may take months to complete the checklist, but when you both agree that the activities have been completed, send a copy to your human resources department to be added to the specialist's personnel file. Use this checklist a couple of times and then add or change items, if needed.

Employment Specialist Orientation Checklist

☐ Read *Supported Employment* (this book).

☐ View IPS Supported Employment videos found at www.dartmouth.edu/~ips. Select "Resources," and then select "Videos."

☐ Shadow another employment specialist (at least four hours).

☐ Shadow a case manager (at least four hours).

☐ Shadow a VR counselor (at least four hours).

☐ Job-develop with supervisor (at least twice during the first month, and then monthly for first six months).

☐ Attend a mental health treatment meeting with supervisor.

☐ Work on career profile with supervisor (two client contacts).

☐ Plan for learning about mental illnesses: _____

_____

_____

_____	_____
Employment specialist signature	date completed
_____	_____
IPS supervisor signature	date completed

Remember, this checklist is just to help new employment specialists get started. You will spend a significant amount of time over the first six to twelve months helping these employees learn, and you'll continue to help them learn throughout their tenure as an employment specialist.

Individual Supervision as a Teaching Tool
During individual supervision, you can help people learn on a case-by-case basis. Let employment specialists identify clients that they want help thinking about, but also use this time to talk about areas in which you think a particular specialist

needs help. For example, if specialists do not seem to be working with families, help them review their caseload to consider which clients might be okay with involving a family member. Ask them how they would discuss the idea with their client, and offer to be present at the first family meeting. Sometimes when a task is avoided, it's because the specialist isn't sure how to do it—so offer to help.

We recommend weekly individual supervision for new specialists. After someone has been working for a year and appears to be doing well, you might decide to reduce supervision to once or twice each month, but don't stop altogether. Individual supervision is a way for you to keep working on *your* relationships with people on your team.

Finally, individual supervision can be another way to help people stay interested in their jobs. You can occasionally use that time to talk to each person about his or her interests. For example, a person who is very interested in job development might want to join a group like the Chamber of Commerce to increase his or her interactions with employers. Another person might want more motivational interviewing training. Also, be sure to take time to point out accomplishments and reinforce the value of each person's work. For example, "Ten months ago, Ryan was homeless. Now he has his own place to live and he's working. You were part of that. Congratulations. Your work has a real impact on people's lives."

The IPS Supervisor as Quality Assurance Manager

At the beginning of this chapter, we noted that supervisors have three roles to maintain: teacher, quality assurance manager, and liaison. In order to have a high-performing program, supervisors must monitor key outcomes to determine areas for celebration and areas for improvement. In this section, we'll talk about some strategies for selecting outcomes, collecting data, and using outcomes. Some of the ideas we'll describe are taken from an article by Gary Bond, Ph.D. To read the entire article, go to http://dartmouth.edu/~ips. Select "Free Newsletter." Select "Previous Newsletters," then select "Winter 2009."

You will need some outcomes that reflect how the program is doing as a whole, but you will also want to collect data that provide information about individual practitioners. Let's begin by focusing on program outcomes.

Selecting and Monitoring Program Outcomes

You may be required to monitor particular outcomes for agencies, such as state vocational rehabilitation or CARF (the Commission on Accreditation of Rehabilitation Facilities) for certification or funding purposes. But, since data are only valuable if they are accurate, we suggest that you think about a manageable number of outcomes and, to the extent possible, focus on data that are relatively simple to collect. If you try to monitor a great number of outcomes at once, or outcomes that are difficult to track, the quality of the information will likely drop.

We recommend collecting information each month. Again, information is only helpful if it is accurate. It is difficult for people to remember what happened two or three months ago, so collect information on a monthly basis, even if you only plan to write quarterly reports. This will also make your life easier when it is time for those quarterly reports because you will have the information you need at your fingertips. Here are some outcomes that are typical for an IPS supported employment program to track:

- ☐ number of people in the IPS program
- ☐ number of new referrals to the IPS program
- ☐ number (and percent) of people who have competitive jobs (see the definition of *competitive jobs* in chapter 2)
- ☐ number of clients who are enrolled in education or technical training programs (not work adjustment programs or training programs for people with disabilities)
- ☐ number of job starts
- ☐ number of working people who have been transitioned off the IPS supported employment caseload (usually after one year of successful work)
- ☐ number of unemployed people who have transitioned off the IPS supported employment caseload

Develop systems that will help you collect some of the information in real time. For example, if you receive copies of all referrals to the program, keep a running count of new referrals each month. If you ask your team to use the Job Start Report, Job Ending Report, and Education Experience Report to update the career profile, also ask them to put a copy of these forms in your mailbox before filing the originals. This will give you information about the number of job starts and job endings, the number of clients who held jobs during the month, and the number of people who entered or exited education programs. You should also plan to sign off on all program closure documents, which will provide you with information about people who are transitioning off the caseload.

Now think about setting a benchmark for competitive employment. IPS programs commonly have 40–50 percent employment at any given time. Some teams have even managed to maintain higher rates in spite of bad economies. But set goals that are realistic. For example, if your program is less than a year old, set a goal of 20 percent. If your current employment rate is 25 percent, set a goal of 30 percent for the next six months. The benchmark helps the team figure out whether or not things are going well. You might also set a benchmark for job starts. On average, two to three job starts per employment specialist, per quarter, is an achievable goal. Some people on the team may exceed that goal.

Periodically, you may also wish to monitor some process outcomes. These are not the same as client outcomes (such as the number of people working or number of people in school); rather, they can give you information about the *way* services are provided. For example, you may occasionally ask employment specialists to track the time that they spend in the community. Examples of other process measures include number of employer contacts per week or types of follow-along supports.

Using Program Data

When you are looking at program data, look not only at the most recent quarter but also the past year. See if you can determine any trends. Do you see the number of job starts rising? Do you see the number of referrals falling? Use the information to pinpoint areas that need improvement and devise a plan to improve the outcome. (Remember that job starts tend to fall a bit from mid-December through February.)

Example:

A team leader, Allen, noticed that over the past six months job starts were good (an average of 2.5 per employment specialist, per quarter), but the overall employment rate for the team was lower than usual (38 percent). Because he didn't see an increase in new referrals or working people transitioning off the team, he began to wonder if a large number of people were losing jobs. He reviewed job ending reports for the last quarter, and it did seem as though quite a few people were losing jobs. Allen brought the outcomes to a unit meeting, where he began by congratulating the team on the number of job starts. He then explained that the overall rate of employment was lower than usual and he suggested that it might be due to job loss. He shared copies of the job ending reports with the team so they could see the number of clients who had been losing their jobs.

The team wasn't sure if this was something over which they had control, but they agreed to focus on follow-along supports for the next two quarters to see if they could increase the percent of people working.

Allen developed a simple plan to focus on job supports for the next two quarters. To help the team, Allen used a portion of team meetings to brainstorm job supports for individual clients. He also began to review client records to see if job supports appeared to be individualized and if clients were receiving enough job supports. When it appeared that someone was not receiving the right type or intensity of job supports, he met with the client and employment specialist to review the follow-along plan. He also attended mental health team meetings to talk about people who were working.

Allen's Plan to Help the Team Improve Job Retention

1. *When someone gets a job, have a team discussion during the vocational unit meeting to talk about the person's work history, strengths, new job, and so on. Help anticipate possible problems. Brainstorm job supports.*

2. *Review records for working people (four to five each month) to review supports provided. Discuss with employment specialist assigned to each person.*

3. *Attend mental health treatment teams at least once each month with employment specialists. Ask to talk about clients who are working. Ask case managers what they have observed about the person's satisfaction with the job, ability to manage the job, and so on. Review job supports.*

4. *Re-evaluate this plan after two more calendar quarters.*

After one quarter, Allen noticed that the rate of employment was 40 percent. He thought that things were either holding steady or improving a bit. He reviewed job ending forms, and only two people had lost jobs (a couple of others quit their jobs). After two quarters, the employment rate had increased to 44 percent. Allen shared this success with his team and continued the focus on job supports for one additional quarter to ensure that the team was providing individualized job supports.

Remember, the overall goal is to increase the number of clients working successfully and to help them eventually transition from the IPS caseload. You could keep a good employment rate by never encouraging the workers to move beyond

IPS services, but who would that benefit? Also remember that the employment rate will decrease if the program receives a large number of new referrals.

Share Outcomes with Agency Administrators

Be an open book, even when outcomes are not as desired. Every program goes through ups and downs, and most administrators understand this. What will impress them is that you are monitoring outcomes and have a plan to improve them. Share a very brief plan (bullet points are best) explaining the action steps you will try. Also, ask for their help. Your executive director surely knows many businesspeople in town and can introduce you to some of those people, to the board of directors, and so on. Make your requests as specific as possible. For example, "We're trying to increase the number of people who find jobs. We'd like to work with Community Hospital but are unable to make a connection in the human resource department. Do you know anyone who can help us with that?" "Our referrals have been very low. I'm attending mental health team meetings to help with that but wondered if you could help as well. It would be meaningful to the case managers to hear that you care about helping people with work."

Also, be sure to let your administrators know when there is something to celebrate. For example, "We've achieved 55 percent employment on the team. That is a real success for an IPS supported employment team." From time to time, you might ask agency executives to help your team celebrate: "The team is excited about this milestone. It would mean a lot to them to hear from you. Would you be willing to say something to them or send them an email?"

Summary: Using Program-Level Data

Remember, to benefit from the data that you are collecting, complete the following steps:

1. Review data quarterly to look for trends.

2. Share outcomes with the team and ask for their opinions and suggestions.

3. Set goals with the team for improved outcomes.

4. Implement a plan with specific action steps to improve the outcome (written plans are best). Keep it simple. Just focus on one outcome at a time. Also, think about how long you will try the interventions (three months? six months?) before evaluating whether the plan is working.

5. Talk to agency administrators about your plan. Ask for their help and feedback.

6. Evaluate whether or not outcomes have improved to a degree that is satisfactory. If not, determine whether to revise the action plan.

Monitoring Outcomes for Individual Employment Specialists

In addition to gathering information about the team's outcomes, be sure to collect outcomes for individual employment specialists. We said that supervisors must be teachers, but how do you know where to focus your efforts with individuals if you are not tracking outcomes by employment specialist? Below is a sample chart of outcomes for one team. Review it and then see if you can answer the questions that follow.

EMPLOYMENT SPECIALIST	CASELOAD SIZE	NUMBER/ PERCENTAGE OF PEOPLE WORKING IN COMPETITIVE JOBS	NUMBER OF PEOPLE IN SCHOOL	NUMBER/ PERCENTAGE OF PEOPLE PURSUING WORK	NUMBER/ PERCENTAGE OF PEOPLE NOT ENGAGED
Clifton	20	11/55%	0	7/35%	2/10%
Sam	17	3/18%	0	10/59%	4/23%
Sonya	19	7/37%	2	9/47%	1/5%
Shontal	22	10/45%	3	8/36%	1/5%
Team Totals	19.5*	40%	5/6%	34/44%	8/10%
GOAL:	20 or less	50% or more			

*This is the average.

1. Which employment specialist(s) might need help with job development?

2. Is there anyone on the team who could share strategies for job development?

3. How is the team doing with caseload sizes?

4. Is anyone having difficulty engaging new clients?

It is difficult to answer these questions with certainty because some important information may be missing from the table. For example, one specialist may have just received a lot of new referrals. However, the outcomes give the supervisor a place to start. He or she can offer to help employment specialists develop a plan to improve their outcomes. For instance, in the example on the previous page, if Sam really is having trouble engaging people, the supervisor might meet with Sam to ask him why he thinks the four people have not yet engaged and then talk about some ways that she can help. For example, she could offer to go out with him to try to develop relationships with some of his clients. She could also offer to go to a mental health team meeting with Sam to discuss how they might help Sam connect with clients. With regard to job development, she could offer to go into the field to help Sam learn some new strategies, and she might also offer to set Sam up to shadow Clifton, who seems to be doing well in this area. She could also review Sam's employer contact logs with him to help him devise plans to follow up with employers. The supervisor and Sam should set a goal to improve outcomes and discuss the goal regularly to see if things are moving in the right direction.

We also recommend that supervisors share monthly outcomes with the entire team. Some supervisors panic at that idea, thinking that it will upset the team. It's true that some team members will feel uncomfortable at first, but a little healthy competition can help motivate team members to improve their outcomes. Further, the supervisor can explain that everyone on the team should try to help each other. For example, "We're all in this together, and we can help each other. If someone else has a lower employment rate, you can offer to make some employer introductions or share some of your job search strategies. We're all going to learn together and improve together."

Holding People Accountable

It's your job as a supervisor to set expectations and then to hold employees accountable to those expectations. Make sure that you communicate clearly and consistently. Diane Erkens, an IPS supervisor from Minnesota, talks about how she sets expectations for time spent in the community:

■ ■ ■

I make it an expectation that services are scheduled in the community. I tell specialists that if they don't have a meeting scheduled or if someone cancels, they should get out there and talk to employers or pick up applications. If a specialist was planning to meet someone in a coffee shop or library and that appointment doesn't happen, the specialist should talk to the staff there about the opportunities at that business. I tell my staff that going out in the community helps us fight stigma. Meeting people in the community, letting people in town see that we are working with regular people who are their neighbors or church members, makes a difference. For the client, it also feels like our services are a part of normal life.

I try to set the expectation right from the beginning. We tell applicants during the interview that the job requires independence and that the person hired would be expected to be in the community at least 85 percent of the time. When a new employment specialist begins, he or she goes out with each employment specialist on the team to see what their days are like. They see it as an expectation right from the beginning. Field mentoring is another way to demonstrate that the work happens in the community.

You have to trust your employment specialists. Even though my team is not in the office, I know they are working hard because I hear about the work that they are doing during supervision and I also see the results in our outcomes. However, we also have a sign-out sheet so we know where specialists are throughout the day (this is also for safety). And occasionally I'll call consumers [clients] to ask how their services are going. That provides me with more feedback about the quality and intensity of services provided.

Make sure that job descriptions clearly state the expectations that you have for specialists. The CD-ROM includes a sample job description for employment specialists. Include things like expectations for number of clients working, time spent in the community, rapid responses to employer needs, number of employer contacts each week, level of collaboration with mental health team members and VR, and ability to help clients find jobs that are good matches. Discuss these expectations with team members routinely, and comment on these areas in performance evaluations. If someone is having trouble, don't let a few months go by before you deal with the issue. Meet with people right away to develop a plan for improvement.

When you have team members who are good at their jobs, make sure to recognize that. Tell them that you appreciate their performance. Ask if they would like to work on specific areas or gain certain types of experience. For example, one person might like opportunities to mentor a new employment specialist while another might like opportunities to do public speaking. Help talented employment specialists build their skills and their résumés.

Unfortunately, not everyone is cut out to be an employment specialist. If you work hard to help a person improve, but he or she is not able to make significant changes over a reasonable period of time, your responsibility is to talk with your human resource department and help the person move on. We have worked with many programs that had poor outcomes simply because the wrong people had been hired and the agency was reluctant to take action. These programs were not able to make significant improvements until there was staff turnover. If someone on your team does not appear to be a good fit, you may encourage the person to consider another job at the agency. For example, there may be another position that fits the person's strengths and would be a better match for him or her. If not, you may need to let the person go. An employment specialist who is not helping clients to work in competitive jobs is not carrying out the essential duties of the job. Letting someone go can be a difficult situation, but remember that you are in charge of quality and that many clients depend on your program. Ask for close supervision if you feel that you may need to eventually let someone go. Be sure to follow agency personnel guidelines.

Here are some tools you have to assess whether employment specialists are providing good services:

- ☐ field mentoring (observation and assessment of skills)
- ☐ chart reviews
- ☐ discussions about clients and employers during individual and group supervision (employment team meetings)
- ☐ feedback from mental health team leaders

Duplicating this page is illegal. Do not copy this material without written permission from the publisher.

179

☐ feedback from clients (talk to clients about their experiences)

☐ employer contact logs (is the person learning about businesses, keeping in touch with businesses over time?)

☐ individual employment specialist outcomes

☐ agency information technology (IT) reports regarding time spent in the community

Hiring Employment Specialists

When hiring employment specialists, many supervisors report that they attempt to hire people who have marketing or sales experience. Others try to hire people who have been employers in the past, and still others seek people who have a background in mental health. Obviously, all of these experiences would be helpful to an employment specialist, though it is usually quite difficult to find one person with all of these backgrounds.

Another approach is to think about the personality type of a successful employment specialist.

For example:

A RECOVERY-ORIENTED CANDIDATE IS SOMEONE WHO	➡ is hopeful about every person's ability to succeed in employment ➡ is open-minded about helping people move into competitive jobs, regardless of active substance use disorders ➡ believes that work can help people manage mental illnesses ➡ believes that people learn and grow from their experiences
A CREATIVE PROBLEM-SOLVER MIGHT	➡ be someone who can think of more than one possible solution to a problem ➡ ask questions to learn more about a particular problem
A CANDIDATE WHO IS GENUINELY INTERESTED IN THE JOB	➡ would attempt to learn about IPS supported employment before the interview (interviewers can provide the link to the Dartmouth Web page for supported employment when scheduling the interview. The link is www.dartmouth.edu/~ips) ➡ would ask questions about the job and their potential job duties
A CANDIDATE WHO WOULD BE A GOOD JOB DEVELOPER	➡ would present himself or herself in a professional and confident manner ➡ may have a gregarious, "sales" personality or may be quiet, yet persistent ➡ would be a good listener—interested in learning about other people

Some supervisors have asked about good interview questions to ask potential employment specialists. In response, a group of IPS supported employment trainers—Barbara Bach, Nicole Clevenger, Joseph Croegaert, and Tony Gantenbein—helped us brainstorm the following list of questions. After each question are suggestions for things that interviewers can listen for.

1. Did you have a chance to read about IPS supported employment? Based on that, what do you think a typical day as an employment specialist would be like? While setting up the interview, share the following Web site with the candidate: http://www.dartmouth.edu/~ips.

   Was the candidate interested enough to read about IPS? Does the person have a good understanding of the job—does he or she know what he or she is applying for?

2. What would you enjoy about this job? What would you *not* enjoy about this job?

   Does the person have a good understanding of the job? Is the candidate able to provide a thoughtful, honest response about parts of the job he or she would not enjoy?

3. How do you go about finding jobs for yourself?

   What type of job search skills does the person already possess? Does the person use networking as one strategy?

4. What would you do if one of your clients began missing appointments?

   Does the candidate seem to blame the client or is the candidate using a problem-solving approach?

5. What do you think about helping people with active substance use problems find employment?

   Does the person have a determined opinion about waiting for people to become sober? If so, how does the candidate respond to information from the interviewer about zero exclusion?

6. What would be your expectations for the people you would serve?

   Does the candidate have ideas such as "People have to be working as hard as I am on the job search"?

7. How would you learn about employers and job opportunities within this community?

   Does the person have some creative ideas? Does the candidate think of ways to get out of the office to meet employers or does the candidate suggest Web sites only?

8. How would you build credibility and strengthen relationships with employers?

   Does the person have ideas such as using face-to-face meetings, listening to what is important to the employer, and following through with next steps?

9. Role-play: Candidate role-plays an employment specialist going back to a restaurant after a client has been working for one week. The manager reports that the client is too slow.

   Does the candidate try to ask questions to figure out what is going on? Does the candidate try to figure out how the client's slow work speed is affecting the business? Does the candidate listen carefully to the employer to learn what is important to the job? What type of solutions does the candidate propose—more than one?

10. Why do you think it would be important to stay in close contact with the mental health team? With rehabilitation counselors from vocational rehabilitation?

    Does the candidate understand how to work as a team member?

11. What do you hope to be doing in five years?

    Does this job really fit the person's work interests?

12. For candidates who do not have mental health experience but who are final candidates for the job, offer to let them shadow an employment specialist for a few hours. Ensure that the employment specialist will be working in the community, visiting people at their homes, and so on. (Be sure to have completed releases in advance of going out with the candidate.)

    Does the candidate think this type of work will be enjoyable? Does it feel okay to go into people's homes? Is the candidate willing to spend the work-day out and about, rather than in an office?

13. For other individuals who are finalists for the job, offer to let them shadow an employment specialist who is making some employer contacts. (Be sure to have completed releases in advance if talking about specific clients or meeting clients.)

    Does the candidate think job development would be enjoyable? Does the candidate feel confident in being able to develop good job development skills over time? Does the person understand that job development would be part of his or her weekly responsibilities?

The IPS Supervisor as Liaison

To function properly, IPS supported employment programs need good relationships with mental health teams, state VR offices, and agency administrators. In this section, we'll discuss how supervisors can help build these relationships.

Building Relationships with Mental Health Treatment Teams

Supervisors can help build relationships with mental health treatment teams by attending those team meetings periodically, for example, once a month. They can demonstrate ways to engage the team in conversations about ideas for good job matches and job supports. They can also explain the IPS supported employment approach. For example, if the team doesn't understand why the employment specialist can't help out with case management work, the supervisor can explain that when employment specialists are pulled in too many directions, clients stop getting new jobs. They can also explain that dedication to employment work is a requirement of the job because it leads to positive outcomes.

IPS supervisors can also regularly meet with individual mental health supervisors to check in. For example, is the mental health supervisor happy with the amount of collaboration going on? Is the supervisor confident in the specialist's ability to provide individualized services? When people are referred to the program, does the employment specialist respond quickly? Does the specialist ever discourage referrals? The IPS supervisor can also ask for help. For example, the IPS supervisor might mention that case managers are not returning phone calls to the specialist. Would the mental health supervisor be willing to talk to his or her team about the importance of returning calls within a day? Or the IPS supervisor might talk to the mental health supervisor about ways to support the employment specialist during treatment team meetings.

Focus on Collaboration with Vocational Rehabilitation

We urge you to build a strong relationship with your VR office. Some research indicates that people who receive both vocational rehabilitation and IPS supported employment services have better employment outcomes than people who only receive one service. The mission of both agencies is to help people with competitive employment. Ask to meet with the local VR supervisor to talk about how you can help each other with outcomes. Consider bringing your clinical director or executive director to the meeting to demonstrate that your agency is serious about wanting to strengthen the relationship. Try to stay positive during the meeting. Focus on the future, rather than on past difficulties.

Here are some strategies that programs have used to improve their working relationship with VR staff:

- In some areas, VR supervisors can identify one or two liaisons to work with the IPS supported employment program. These liaisons are rehabilitation counselors who want to work with people who have severe mental illnesses. The liaisons receive all, or most, of the referrals to the IPS supported employment program and work closely with the program.

- Schedule monthly meetings between VR counselors and the IPS supported employment specialists to discuss cases and possible referrals. VR counselors and employment specialists can also discuss services that will be provided in the coming month. Further, the IPS team can benefit from the rehabilitation counselors' knowledge of local employers, medical issues, and so on. It is particularly helpful if both the VR and the IPS supervisor attend this meeting each month.

- Office space at the mental health agency for rehabilitation counselors is helpful. Meeting with clients at the mental health center can help rehabilitation counselors cut down on missed appointments because it is a familiar environment to clients. Sharing office space also helps to build relationships between the two programs because it provides opportunities for practitioners to talk frequently. When the VR counselors are present, remember to invite them to workplace celebrations such as baby showers or retirement parties. This can help the VR counselors feel that they are part of the team. Remember that rehabilitation counselors need private space to meet with clients, along with an Internet connection, access to a copier, and so forth.

- Develop agreements to try new approaches. Discuss eliminating vocational evaluations and situational assessments. Provide the VR office with information about IPS supported employment principles and the research supporting its superior outcomes. At some point, ask the VR supervisor and counselors if they would be willing to serve some clients with alcohol or drug problems. If counselors feel very uncomfortable with this, wait until your relationship is stronger and then ask again. Offer to start small. In other words, you might not refer everyone with a substance use problem right away. Let the counselors gain confidence in this area as they experience success with some people.

- Invite rehabilitation counselors to occasionally attend the IPS supported employment unit meeting or mental health treatment team meeting. Rehabilitation counselors have high caseloads and may not be able to attend frequently, but many say they appreciate the opportunity to interact with other people who are making treatment recommendations to their clients. Talk to agency administrators about releases so that the rehabilitation counselors can participate fully in the meeting. For instance, rehabilitation counselors might sign a release similar to the one that CARF reviewers or consultants use when they visit your agency.

Remember to be patient. IPS supported employment principles represent a significant change of course for many rehabilitation counselors. Even so, we have seen many relationships improve over time.

Learn about VR policies and practices. Be sure you understand the type and frequency of documentation that rehabilitation counselors need from your program. Also, try to understand the pressures that rehabilitation counselors are under. Remember, vocational rehabilitation counselors are evaluated, in part, by the number of people who work at competitive jobs. When VR counselors don't do something that you think they should, remember they are working in a different system that you may not understand entirely. Ask to talk about the situation and begin by asking questions to understand the counselor's point of view.

Educate and Involve Agency Administrators

IPS supervisors keep agency administrators interested and involved in IPS supported employment. An executive director or executive administration team that is invested in competitive jobs for clients is invaluable. But chances are that your agency administrators don't understand the details of employment for clients. They're also probably very busy. So try to educate them, and be prepared to educate them in brief spurts. For example, ask to attend an agency administration meeting once a quarter to provide a short (ten-minute) update. Prepare a one-page report that is easy to read (for example, use bullet points or simple tables). Include successes, areas for improvement, and requests for help in the report.

Example of program update:

IPS Supported Employment Program Update
March 20XX

Program Strengths:	▶ 50 percent rate of competitive employment on the team. This is considered an outstanding outcome for a program like ours.
	▶ Growing number of referrals. Clients and mental health practitioners believe that work is a critical component of recovery.
	▶ Strong relationship with our local VR office.
Areas for Improvement:	▶ Caseloads are high due to the increase in referrals. We have a waiting list of 32 people who want to work. Some people lose interest in work if left on a waiting list for too long.
Ways Administration Can Help:	▶ Help us think about resources to hire another employment specialist.
	▶ Help us clear up a small billing problem between our billing department and VR.

Agency administrators need to understand the importance of work in people's lives. Help them hear directly from working people about how work has changed their lives. Ask clients to speak about their jobs to administrators. Take your executive director out to visit (with permission) a person on the job—seeing is believing. Once the executive team has stories and firsthand experiences with people who have been transformed by work, they will be in a much better position to champion the IPS program with their board and with funders. They will also be more likely to help the program sustain positions when the budget is tight.

SUMMARY

As a supervisor, you play a critical role in ensuring quality services for people who want to work. Your number one role is to make sure that the program is able to help most clients find satisfying jobs. To do that, you must be prepared to teach staff how to develop jobs, interact with clients, and provide good job supports. You must also monitor key outcomes and use those outcomes to implement program improvements. At times, you will need to hold people accountable to certain job expectations. Finally, your job includes building relationships between other departments and agencies such as mental health teams, agency administrators, and your local VR office.

• • •

TOOLS FOR IPS SUPPORTED EMPLOYMENT SUPERVISION:

- [21] Sample Employment Specialist Job Description
- [22] Sample IPS Supported Employment Supervisor Job Description
- • Job development videos. Go to http://dartmouth.edu~ips. Select "Resources." Select "Videos." Select "IPS Supported Employment Strategies That Work," then "Job Development."
- [23] Field Mentoring Log for Job Development
- [24] Field Mentoring Log for Skills Development
- [25] IPS Supported Employment Supervision Record
- [26] Employment Specialist Orientation Checklist
- [16] IPS Supervisor's Guide to Individualized Follow-Along Plans

Duplicating this page is illegal. Do not copy this material without written permission from the publisher.

187

Mentdal Health Practitioners and Employment

Please note: This chapter explores the role of practitioners on the mental health treatment team. Others (such as clinical supervisors, agency administrators, and family members) should also read this to learn how mental health practitioners can help people with employment goals.

Case managers, substance abuse counselors, psychiatrists, and other practitioners have a key role in helping people with mental illnesses return to work. The main goal of the mental health system is to ensure that clients have opportunities to live, learn, work, and participate fully in their communities. Helping clients consider employment can open up doors for people to do those things. It will change people's lives and move them toward recovery in ways that can be difficult to imagine. Here's how going back to work transformed the life of a woman named Becky:

■ ■ ■

Everybody works. So when a person is unemployed, it feels very isolating. Like you don't fit in. Helping people get jobs is more than just helping them with work—it can change the way that someone thinks about herself. A friend of mine talks about how she felt the first time that she paid for groceries with cash that she earned instead of food stamps. She said that no one could tell her how to spend the money that she earned.

Employment gives you a purpose. You have a goal. It gives you reason to get out of bed in the morning and a sense of accomplishment at the end of the day.

continued next page

Furthermore, disability benefits are designed for survival and not much more. You can't get ahead on benefits. Employment is a way to make your life better. You can move to a nicer place or buy things that are important to you and have hobbies or buy things for your children. That's a better quality of life.

If I were to give advice to mental health practitioners, I would say that they can help by seeing each person as an individual with strengths. It's important to recognize that every person has something to contribute. By feeling hopeful for their client's ability to do well at a job, they can give hope to their clients. Above all, hope is the key.

It's critical not to evaluate which clients you think can or can't work. No one can accurately predict whether a particular individual can succeed at work. Clients surprise practitioners all the time with unexpected successes. The IPS supported employment research studies also surprised many people when high numbers of people with severe mental illnesses went back to work. Researchers found that interest in employment was an important predictor of success. Talk to everyone on your caseload about work—you never know who may be interested. Also, try talking to people as soon as they begin to receive services from the mental health center. It's important that your clients know from the start that you are there to help with recovery, not just illness management. Even when people are very ill, you can still make hopeful comments such as "when you go back to work" and "if you decide to get a job."

Remember, however, that some clients need time to think about making a change like going back to work. You probably know people who haven't thought about work for years. Some clients report that they stopped thinking about themselves as workers because no one in their lives saw them as workers. Those people may need to think and talk about work in order to rekindle their interest. Mental health workers who have a high percentage of working people on their caseloads report that they approach the issue of work more than once with each client. In fact, they say that they bring up work on a regular basis. Again, Becky shares her experiences working with a therapist who kept talking about work:

I am glad that my therapist did keep talking about work, but not pushing me before I thought I was ready, because it kept me thinking about it. When I did go to work, I was having a lot of problems in my life and my therapist wasn't sure the timing was right, but he let me make the decision, and he supported me for more than three years while I worked at that job. So I think just discussing work is the way to plant the seed in someone's mind. Making them feel more confident and comfortable with the idea that they can succeed. And if it doesn't work for them, it is not the end of the world. They will have learned that "that's not the one for me" and have someone to support them. A couple of jobs later, I am still having problems with working because of issues and symptoms, but my therapist is the one I can count on to keep me trying. I have a part-time job that is very flexible and it seems to be working better.

Methods to Encourage Client Involvement in IPS Programs

In the following sections, we'll describe methods for helping clients consider employment as well as ways to make referrals to IPS supported employment programs. These sections include

1. Helping people who have a strong interest in working

2. Encouraging people who lack confidence

3. Listening to people who are ambivalent about work

4. Talking with people who don't want to work

5. Supporting clients who work on their own

6. Staying involved after a referral

7. Working with employment specialists

These strategies are based on the person's current level of commitment to employment and confidence about work. Below are some statements a person might make based on his or her commitment and confidence level:

- "I've been trying to work on my own and haven't been successful, but I want a job."

- "I'm happy that you are talking to me about work. I want to find out if I can work."

- "I'm not sure if I want to work. Some days it sounds good and other days it doesn't sound so good." Or a person may say, "I like the general idea, but the negative aspects of working bother me."

- "I don't want to work." Or, "I can't work."

In IPS supported employment, *readiness* does not refer to symptoms, substance use, hygiene, treatment compliance, or other such issues. Rather, readiness is all about the client's preference for work. We also believe that clients are capable of making the best choices for themselves if they receive accurate information, have opportunities to think about their values and long-term goals, and have the chance to talk through the pros and cons of such a life-changing decision as going back to work.

Helping People Who Have a Strong Interest in Working

If you have heard a person making comments to the effect of, "I've been trying to work on my own and haven't been successful, but I still want a job," this person may benefit from IPS services. You may have people on your caseload who frequently lose jobs or who apply for jobs without getting hired. These attempts to achieve a working life are a concrete demonstration of interest in employment. Sometimes people do things that are ineffective, such as applying for work with dirty hair and clothes. But, just getting into the community and looking for a job is evidence that the person is interested in working. People who have been trying on their own are great candidates for IPS supported employment. With extra assistance and guidance from an employment specialist, these people are likely to be successful at work.

When you observe that someone is trying but needs extra help, don't wait to make an IPS supported employment referral. If too much time passes, some people will become discouraged and lose interest in working. Offer IPS supported employment services as soon as you believe a client wants help in order to work. Provide information about the program and offer a joint meeting with an employment specialist so the person can learn more about the program. For example, offer to invite an employment specialist to the first fifteen minutes of your next appointment. After the specialist leaves, ask the person for his or her reaction to the services offered by the specialist. What would be the advantages to working with the specialist? The disadvantages?

Encouraging People Who Lack Confidence

If someone on your caseload says something such as, "I'm happy that you are talking to me about work, but I'm not sure that I can work," express your belief that the person has skills and strengths to bring to the workplace. Some clients may have always been interested in work but assumed that they couldn't because of mental illness, low expectations from others, fear of losing benefits, a criminal record, or the difficulties of finding a job. When you begin to talk about work with these people, they may express interest right away. You could respond by trying to find out if there is information that these individuals need, or concerns that they need to talk through before moving ahead to return to work. Before rushing to make a referral, ask questions such as, "How will your life be different if you get a job?" "What would be the good things about working?" "The not-so-good things?" "What are your concerns about getting a job?" "What are your hopes for a job?" In some cases, you may be able to talk through these issues in one or two appointments.

If the person feels that the good things about work outweigh the risks, it's time to make a referral. Provide information about IPS supported employment and make the referral quickly.

Listening to People Who Are Ambivalent about Work

You may hear clients say, "I'm not sure if I want to work. Some days it sounds good and other days it doesn't sound so good." Or they may say, "I like the general idea but the negative aspects of working bother me." Some people have a hard time deciding whether or not they want to go ahead with getting a job. Many people aren't sure if going to work will actually improve the quality of their lives. No one can make that assessment for them. Each individual knows himself or herself best and is best able to decide if work is something that will improve his or her life.

Don't Try to Convince People Who Are Ambivalent about Work

Mental health practitioners can help not by trying to convince the person that work is positive, but by helping the person think through the pros and cons of going to work. Mental health workers are best able to do this by remaining

Duplicating this page is illegal. Do not copy this material without written permission from the publisher.

193

neutral. Try not to push people toward work. Just let clients know that you believe they have strengths, skills, and abilities. During your discussions, do your best to share these ideas:

- I believe you can work.

- Only you know if this is the right time to go to work.

- It's your choice. Only you can make the right decision for you.

Remember that in many cultures, adults are expected to work. It can be embarrassing for people to admit that they might not want to work. Some people will say "yes" because work is valued in our culture or because they are afraid to close the door on the subject by saying "no." In truth, they may not be sure exactly how they feel about getting a job. If you refer those clients to IPS supported employment programs, there is a good chance that they won't engage with an employment specialist or that they will quickly drop out of the program. Tell people that if they want to go to work now, you will make a referral right away. But if they would like more time to think about work, that's fine as well. In the following example, Ted describes how important it was to have someone really listen to his concerns and also to have time to reflect before making decisions:

▪▪▪

I've worked with great people. They valued my feelings and were very good listeners. That was true for my therapist, VR counselor, and employment specialist. That's important. People with mental illnesses sometimes feel defiant about the social service system because practitioners don't always understand how critical the client's concerns are. So the counselor pushes the person forward when they really need to spend some time connecting to the person's discomfort. Being receptive to how people feel and really good listening skills are gifts!

Clinicians can offer up their best advice, but ultimately I need to make the decision. Sometimes I need time to think about my feelings before I can resolve an issue. Sometimes being a good practitioner means letting the person spend the time they need to rehash something.

Help People Consider the Pros and Cons
of Working if They Are Ambivalent about Work

Some people get stuck as they try to think about all of the positive and negative aspects of working. You can help those people write down their ideas about work so that they have a clear picture of the pros and cons. For example, you could ask them to list the good things about being unemployed. You could also ask them to list the bad things about unemployment. Next, you might suggest that they list the good things about working as well as the bad things about working. By breaking things down, clients may gain some insights into their concerns about work. If nothing else, you will know them better at the end of the process.

Sometimes a good question is more effective than sharing your own beliefs. It is rarely effective to try to convince someone to change. Instead, you can ask questions to help people think about their lives and their goals. In that way, commitment to making changes will come directly from the person, rather than from you. Below are some questions you can use to start conversations about work:

- ☐ Was there a time when you wanted to work? Why was work important to you then? What's changed since then?

- ☐ In what ways would it be good for you to go to work? In what ways might it be not so good for you to go to work?

- ☐ If you decide to work, how would you go about it?

- ☐ You've been talking about wanting a better place to live for a while now. Tell me how unemployment fits into that goal.

- ☐ What would keep you from working? What would help you overcome obstacles to work?

- ☐ How will you know when you are ready to work?

- ☐ When was the last time you tried working? How did that go?

- ☐ What was your favorite job? Why? Least favorite job? Why?

- ☐ What are your reasons for thinking about work now?

- ☐ How could holding a job change the kind of role model that you are for your children? What would be the downside of working and raising kids?

- ☐ You've been having a hard time financially (or, you are saying that you're bored, lonely). Are you hoping that will change in the future? How might it change?

- ☐ If you had an extra $300 or $700 a month, what would you spend it on?

☐ On a scale of 1 to 10, how important is it for you to work? Why are you at a ___ and not a 1? What would need to change for you to move to a ___ (higher number)?

1	2	3	4	5	6	7	8	9	10
Not at all important									Very important

☐ On a scale of 1 to 10, how confident are you that you can succeed at work? Why are you at a ___ and not a 1? What would need to change for you to move to a ___ (higher number)?

1	2	3	4	5	6	7	8	9	10
Not at all important									Very important

☐ How would your life be different if you worked? What would be the positive and negative effects on your finances? your friends and family? your time? how you feel about yourself? how you feel about your life?

☐ What would need to change in your life for you to consider seeking employment?

Reframe Past Experiences When People Are Ambivalent about Work

Some people may feel that work would improve their lives but believe they don't have the skills or abilities to find or keep a job. It's possible that they might have tried working in the past without success. Help clients reframe past work experiences by thinking about aspects of the job that they did well. For example, if someone has found many jobs but has not been able to keep them, you could point out that most people have difficulty getting jobs and that he or she must have a real knack for doing so. It's likely that the person is able to present himself or herself well and is resourceful and persistent. You could ask the person for the secret to success: "How were you so successful at job finding?" You could then move on to talk about how the person managed to keep jobs for even a short duration of time. Chances are that the person was using some skills that can be useful in the future. However, as you are affirming the person's skills, try not to start cheerleading. Instead, point out true accomplishments in a matter-of-fact way. Remember that if clients feel you are pushing them to go back to work, their natural reaction will be to worry about the reasons that they might not benefit from a job.

Other people may lack confidence about work because they are afraid their symptoms would interfere with a job. Ask them to tell you about their specific concerns. You might also let them know that most people with mental illness are able to find jobs through IPS supported employment programs and that work seems to help people feel better about themselves and more satisfied with their lives. You could also ask an employment specialist to sit in a meeting with you and the client and share examples of job supports or careful job matching to illustrate that having help can make a difference.

Share Relevant Information When People Are Ambivalent about Work
In addition to helping clients explore their feelings about jobs, you may need to help them get accurate information about work-related issues. Following are some areas in which many clients, and even practitioners, often lack correct information:

Benefits and Work: Many clients are fearful of losing their benefits (that is, Social Security benefits, medical benefits, housing vouchers, welfare, food stamps, and so on) if they go back to work. The truth is that most people can work (at least part time) and keep all or some of their benefits. It's important for everyone who receives benefits to learn how a job can affect their overall income and health benefits. Try not to apply general information, as the rules are different based on the type and combination of benefits a particular individual receives. Ask your IPS supported employment specialist or local VR counselor how to refer people for individualized benefits counseling.

Supports for Work: Some clients feel dissatisfied with vocational services they have received in the past and don't want to repeat those experiences. Try to explain how IPS supported employment differs from traditional services. For example, in IPS it isn't necessary to participate in prevocational programs; instead, employment specialists help people begin looking for a job right away.

Many people dread searching for a job and still others fear losing a job. Explain that an employment specialist is available to work side by side with clients to help them find jobs. Also, they can choose to have the specialist speak to employers on their behalf to help them find jobs and also to help them stay employed.

Many clients are attracted to the IPS principle about client choice. Explain that the program will help them to find jobs that match their preferences. Tell them that they will work with the employment specialist to find a job that is a good fit. If individuals are interested in learning more about IPS supported employment, ask an employment specialist to sit in on the next appointment.

Overcoming Obstacles to Work: There are numerous inspirational stories about people with mental illnesses who have overcome barriers to go to work. Almost every person with severe mental illness who is working has an interesting story to tell. Hearing clients talk about their return to work can be motivating and useful to others who are not sure how they would overcome barriers. If you know someone who would be willing to share his or her story with another client, talk with your supervisor about your agency's rules for confidentiality and your plans to set up a meeting. Then ask your client if he or she would like you to invite the working person to your next appointment. Be present for this conversation so that you can help facilitate the discussion about working around obstacles.

Offer IPS as Ambivalence about Work Is Resolved

Over time, you will find that many clients will resolve their ambivalence about work and decide to take action. When someone on your caseload begins to feel that the benefits of work outweigh the negative aspects of working, it is a good time to make a referral to IPS supported employment. Hopeful feelings about overcoming barriers to work are another sign that a client may be ready for IPS supported employment. In this case, offer to set up a meeting with an employment specialist so the person can learn more about IPS supported employment or more about jobs in the community. Also, offer to attend this meeting with the client. Finally, be sure to offer a referral if you hear that clients have been taking steps on their own to find a job, even if the steps are small.

Continue to talk about work and help clients with their concerns even after you have made the referral. Ask them what they think about the program. Ask how it feels to actually be in the middle of a job search. What do they hope for in a job? What, if any, concerns, do they have about starting a new job? There is always a danger that people can slide backward without enough support.

Talking with People Who Don't Want to Work

Some clients will say, "I don't want to work" or "I can't work." Indeed, it's likely that some people on your caseload will be positive that they don't want to work. You may even have noticed that the more you encourage these individuals to think about a job, the more unyielding they become. When clients say that they don't want to work, it's time to step back. Take a very gentle approach to talking about jobs. Avoid trying to convince or lead. Instead, help them think about the vision that they have for life, and whether or not work fits with their values and goals.

There are several reasons that a person may not be willing to think about the possibility of work:

- Some people feel hopeless about making any kind of change in their lives. It may be up to the practitioner to help bring hope to the person. For example, practitioners could share beliefs such as "I'm sure you are going to feel better than you feel now," "I think you are a stronger person than you realize," or "I am confident you will overcome the problems you are struggling with now."

- The person may not see the negative consequences of being unemployed. For example, although you may feel frustrated that a particular person complains of boredom month after month, it may not occur to that person that work is a good way to stay busy and involved in the community.

- The person may feel that he or she doesn't have the ability to find and keep a job. Some people have been told that work can increase the symptoms of their illness (even though the evidence does not support this notion). Sometimes clients infer that they aren't capable of working because nobody asks them if they are interested in a job. Finally, some clients may just feel overwhelmed at the idea of managing mental illnesses and holding down jobs.

- Other people may have simply accepted their lives as they are. Many people with mental illnesses have unstructured days with little social or productive activity. Undoubtedly, this is not the life they planned for themselves when they were in high school. Yet when some people first experience the symptoms of mental illness, they become preoccupied with dealing with the crises in their lives. Although problems can lessen over time, people may become accustomed to having less activity in their lives. It's also notable that many of us who are practitioners also begin to accept that some clients have relatively little activity in their lives.

You may discover that some people have misinformation, such as bad information about benefits, available transportation, or services to help with the job search. Sometimes people say "no" to work because they assume you mean a full-time job. Try to help clients gain correct information about these and other concerns. Ask your IPS supported employment program staff for information about issues with which you are not familiar. For instance, the IPS program should be able to tell you how to help the person find benefits information.

When people *aren't even considering* work, it makes little sense to talk about the pros and cons of working. Instead, help these clients think about what they want to get out of life and whether there are any areas of their lives they would like to change. Often, employment will rise to the surface as people think about having more income or something to do with their time. At first it may be hard for people to consider changing their lives, but they will gain momentum because you are hopeful and positive. Be flexible. You may wish to talk about employment, but a particular client might be focused on other interests, such as housing, relationships, hobbies, or learning. It's okay if people go in other directions. Help people think about which goals feel important to them. Over time they may decide that employment is important as well. And if some people decide not to work, that's fine also. Your job isn't to talk people into going to work—just to help them consider all of their options.

Below are some questions that may help clients begin to think about their values and hopes for the future:

- [ ] What do you want your life to look like in three years? In five years? Where will you live? What type of relationships do you hope to have? What do you see yourself doing during the day?
- [ ] Have there been times in your life when work did seem important to you? If so, what changed?
- [ ] What is a typical day for you? What did you do after you woke up yesterday? What did you do later in the day? Are you satisfied with how you spend your days? Is there anything that you would like to change?
- [ ] Are there people you admire who are working?
- [ ] If you decided to work, what kind of job would interest you?
- [ ] What were your goals for your life when you were in high school? How have those goals changed? Why have those goals changed?
- [ ] Describe recovery to me. What will your personal recovery look like? How will you know when you are on the road to recovery?
- [ ] What are your talents? What are you good at?

As you hear people begin to talk about both the good and bad things related to work, you'll know that you've made progress. Signs that the person is starting to consider employment, or to imagine how life would be different if he or she worked, are indications that things are moving forward. Still, don't rush a referral to IPS supported employment yet. Now it's time to patiently help the person begin to weigh the pros and cons of working. Read through the section on page 193, "Listening to People Who Are Ambivalent about Work," to get some ideas that will help the person think about work.

Remember, people may occasionally slide backward and lose interest in talking about the pros and cons of work. That's okay. Help people think about their values and how they want their life to look—work will come up again.

Supporting Clients Who Work on Their Own

Just by talking about work, some people on your caseload will go out and get a job on their own. They may also do pretty well at the job, though most of us require at least some job supports—you probably have at least one person in your life who helps you think through some of your own job issues. Try to remember the last time you were unhappy with an aspect of work or the last time you started a new job. Chances are that you needed support.

If someone on your caseload is employed with only a few concerns, it may not be necessary to refer that person to IPS supported employment. Instead, you can provide support just by talking about the job. Ask specific questions on a regular basis. For example:

- ☐ Has your supervisor given you any feedback lately? What did you think about those comments? What did you say when you got the feedback?

- ☐ Do your job duties ever change? What's the hardest part of your job?

- ☐ Do you like your work? What are your likes and dislikes about the job?

- ☐ Are your co-workers friendly? Do people eat lunch together? Do you eat lunch with them? Do people go out after work? Do you go along?

- ☐ Are you planning to stay at this job? How long do you think you will stay? What would be your reasons for leaving?

The more you help clients describe what is going on at work, the more likely it is that people will come to you to talk through job concerns. If a client begins to have serious difficulty at work, consider a referral to IPS supported employment. IPS programs can help people keep jobs they already have or help people find new jobs. If you aren't sure if it is time for a referral, talk it over with an employment specialist. You could even ask the employment specialist to sit in an appointment with you and the client to see if he or she has any creative ideas to solve the problem without a referral to the IPS program.

Staying Involved after a Referral

Remember that making a big change is not always a straightforward process. People tend to wax and wane a bit in their commitment. Therefore, even after clients decide to go to work, they might lose confidence or interest in the goal.

After you make a referral to the IPS program, plan to stay involved in the work goal. The people you serve probably know and trust you more than the employment specialist, particularly in the beginning. By talking about work during part of every appointment, you are demonstrating your support for their employment goal. Further, you can continue to express your belief that they have strengths and talents to offer an employer.

Another strategy for helping someone stay involved is to work closely with the employment specialist. Set up an appointment for the three of you to brainstorm about jobs or celebrate successes. When that isn't possible, make sure to talk to the employment specialist regularly so you can each reinforce the work that the other is doing.

Working with Employment Specialists

The more that mental health practitioners involve themselves in the vocational process, the more likely it is that their clients will be successful at work. Although the employment specialist will do most of the work to help a person find and keep a job, mental health practitioners also have a role to play. For example, counselors and case managers can reinforce the gains that a client has made through work during their meetings with the person. Mental health practitioners can also help employment specialists think of good ideas for job matches and, on occasion, may tell an employment specialist about a job opening. When a person finds employment, the mental health practitioner may even be part of the job support plan. Helping people with social skills related to work, helping people manage their extra income, or helping them improve their appearance for a job are all important job supports that can be part of a mental health practitioner's role. It's important to communicate frequently with the employment specialist to share information, coordinate efforts to support the employment plan, and celebrate success together.

Tips for Mental Health Supervisors

Incorporating the idea of zero exclusion—that is, anyone who wants to work is eligible for IPS supported employment right away—takes place over time. It is not enough to tell practitioners about zero exclusion and then expect them to put the principle into practice. Helping clients think about work, without cheerleading or pushing, is something of an art. Below are some suggestions for helping your team in this area:

- Review this chapter with practitioners. Ask them to share their ideas and concerns. Don't worry if some people have concerns early on—this is going to be a major change for some people on the team.

- Help practitioners apply these ideas to individual people on their caseload. For example, if a practitioner asks you about someone who is talking about work but never seems to take action, quickly review the section "Listening to People Who Are Ambivalent about Work" on page 193.

- If you use a form to take notes during supervision, add a section on employment to remind yourself to ask about clients' interest in employment. At first practitioners may not be able to answer this question for every client. Encourage them to ask each person directly and to continue asking now and then.

- Put posters and/or IPS supported employment brochures in your meeting rooms. You'll be surprised how helpful visual reminders can be. Posters about IPS supported employment for clients can be ordered from http://www.dartmouth.edu/~ips. Select "Resources." Select "Posters."

- Keep track of the number of people who are either working or engaged in the IPS supported employment program on each practitioner's caseload. You'll find that some practitioners are more skilled at helping people with work than others. Ask those practitioners to share their strategies with others on the team.

- Set the expectation that mental health practitioners will talk about work. Describe that expectation in job descriptions and include training about IPS supported employment in new employee orientation. For example, ask new practitioners to view videos about people going back to work (see "Tools to Help People Consider Employment" on the next page).

. . .

TOOLS TO HELP PEOPLE CONSIDER EMPLOYMENT:

(SP) [27] "So, you may be interested in a job . . ." Worksheet.

- We recommend the videos *3 Faces, 3 Lives* and *Introduction* or *Introduction—Spanish* to hear first-person accounts of using IPS supported employment services. Go to www.dartmouth.edu/~ips. Select "Resources." Select "Videos," then "Introducing IPS Supported Employment."

- Many of the ideas in this chapter were adopted from the stages of change developed by Prochaska, Norcross, and DiClemente. You can learn more about the stages of change, as well as techniques to help people make change, by attending workshops about motivational interviewing. There is also a book called *Motivational Interviewing* (Miller and Rollnick, 2002). Details about this book are included in the Suggested Reading list in this book (page 225) or at www.motivationalinterview.org.

Family Members: What You Need to Know about IPS Supported Employment

Authors' note: This chapter focuses on the role of family members in IPS supported employment. However, other team members, such as IPS supervisors, employment specialists, and addiction and mental health counselors, should also read this chapter to learn how family members can be part of IPS supported employment. They may also use this as a handout (it is included on the CD-ROM for duplication) and as a guide for orienting family members as part of the team.

Many families have watched a family member with mental illness attempt to work independently or with assistance from a vocational program. If that has been your experience, you may be wondering how Individual Placement and Support (IPS) supported employment is different from other employment programs. You may also wonder how you can find an IPS program and how you can support your family member while he or she is pursuing the goal of employment. In this chapter, we'll talk about all of those issues, but before we begin, it is important to state that the term *family* might refer to a parent, child, sibling, spouse, or partner. Family might also include a good friend, clergy member, or other important person. We believe it is up to each person participating in IPS to determine who to include in his or her employment plan.

An Introduction to IPS Supported Employment

In this chapter, you will learn about

1 The relationship between employment and recovery

2 Research that shows IPS is effective

3 The role of state vocational rehabilitation

4 The role of the family in IPS supported employment

5 How to find IPS supported employment programs

6 How to support IPS programs in your state

Employment and Recovery

Many people report that getting a job is a critical component of their recovery. Jobs give people opportunities to rejoin their communities and spend time with other people. Jobs also remind people that they have valuable skills and strengths. In surveys, people who went back to work reported that they felt better about themselves when they were employed, and some people reported that they experienced fewer symptoms while they were working. Not every person with severe mental illness will decide to go back to work. We believe, however, that everyone should have the opportunity to talk about work and decide for themselves if work is a goal that they would like to pursue.

Work is important to me. I needed something to do. When I wasn't working, all I could think about was the time that I had on my hands. Having something to do makes a person's life bearable.

—Mark

Research Shows That IPS Supported Employment Works

IPS is a well-researched approach to helping people who are recovering from mental illnesses. The IPS employment program is effective with individuals of all ages in both urban and rural communities. In fact, regardless of the economy, people with severe mental illnesses are more likely to find jobs if helped by IPS than other types of vocational services. In eleven of eleven studies, people who had access to IPS were more likely to obtain employment. In fact, 61 percent of people in IPS programs obtained jobs, while 23 percent of people using other vocational programs found employment (Bond, Drake, and Becker 2008). Additional studies show that people who found jobs while engaged in IPS programs had success in those jobs over time.

What's different about IPS? IPS program supervisors follow careful procedures to ensure the use of twenty-five key components of successful employment programs. These are described in the IPS Supported Employment Fidelity Scale. (See appendix A and the CD-ROM.) These are all based on research, so we know those programs that follow the procedures will deliver good results.

Another way to conceptualize an IPS program is to think about the seven guiding principles for IPS programs (also reviewed in chapter 2).

IPS SUPPORTED EMPLOYMENT GUIDING PRINCIPLES	OTHER TYPES OF EMPLOYMENT SERVICES
1. All people with severe mental illness who are interested in a job are eligible for IPS.	Many other types of employment programs attempt to assess which people are ready to work and screen out those who appear to have the most significant barriers to employment.
People are not screened out because of symptoms, substance use, hospitalization history, personal presentation, missed mental health appointments, medication nonadherence, work history, or other factors.	Some programs are able to help with a second job. Most are unable to help with more than two jobs or may require the person to meet certain criteria before embarking on another job search.
If job loss occurs, the person is offered immediate assistance with another job. Practitioners and the person talk about lessons learned and try to make a better job match.	
Rationale: Research has demonstrated that interest in employment is so important that it sometimes outweighs other factors.	
2. All IPS participants are offered information about the effects of earned income on benefits (Social Security benefits, housing subsidies, food stamps, and so on) prior to starting a job.	Many employment programs offer benefits planning, at least once.
IPS programs also offer assistance with benefits as individuals face decisions about changes in income or as individuals could benefit from work incentives (programs that are intended to allow people to earn more money without loss of benefits).	
Rationale: People need information to make informed choices about how much they will work if they choose to stay on benefits. Others need to know about strategies for exiting the benefits system.	

continued on next page

IPS SUPPORTED EMPLOYMENT GUIDING PRINCIPLES	OTHER TYPES OF EMPLOYMENT SERVICES
3. Mental health treatment practitioners and employment practitioners work together closely. This includes weekly face-to-face meetings to discuss client goals for employment and to brainstorm strategies to help people reach those goals. Because some people receive services from state vocational rehabilitation (VR) in addition to the IPS program, IPS practitioners meet at least once each month with rehabilitation counselors from VR to ensure that services are delivered in a seamless manner. **Rationale:** Employment outcomes are better when programs use integrated services. Further, people receiving services report that they are confused or frustrated when mental health practitioners, employment specialists, and/or VR counselors give conflicting messages.	Services are often brokered, meaning that people receive mental health services at one agency and vocational services at another. Practitioners do not communicate frequently.
4. Competitive jobs are the goal. Competitive jobs are regular jobs in the community that pay at least minimum wage (or the wage that co-workers are earning), are either part-time or full-time positions, are not jobs that are set aside for people with disabilities, and do not have artificial time limits imposed by the employment program. Some people may choose to begin with school or adult vocational training programs as a way to prepare for a particular job. School and training programs utilized by IPS programs are those that are open to any adult in the community—not just those who have disabilities. **Rationale:** Most people receiving services report that they want to work in competitive jobs.	Some employment programs offer jobs that are created just for people with disabilities or jobs that pay less than minimum wage. They may also offer volunteer work or sheltered workshops because they don't believe people are ready for regular jobs.

continued on next page

IPS SUPPORTED EMPLOYMENT GUIDING PRINCIPLES	OTHER TYPES OF EMPLOYMENT SERVICES
5. The job search is rapid. This means that within a few weeks of a client expressing interest in a job, an employment specialist works with the person to initiate contact with employers. This doesn't mean that people necessarily begin work right away, since it may take time to find a job. Using a rapid job search also means that people are *not* asked to spend time on vocational evaluations, job tryouts, job readiness groups, or any other prework activities prior to starting the job search. **Rationale:** People who have access to a rapid job search are more likely to obtain jobs.	Many employment programs ask people to engage in vocational evaluations (paper and pencil tests), job tryouts, readiness groups, or other preparatory activities before starting the job search. They use a stepwise approach to help people with work. If a person does not succeed at an early step, that person may never graduate to a competitive job search.
6. Client preferences are important. Preferences may refer to the type of work, job location, number of hours worked each week, work shift, disclosure of a disability to an employer, and so forth. Preferences are also related to the way that services are provided, for instance, whether an employment specialist provides job supports at the work site or away from the job. **Rationale:** Using an individualized approach leads to success. Further, when people find jobs that match their preferences, they stay at those jobs longer.	Some employment programs offer limited choices regarding the employment goal and services provided.

continued on next page

IPS SUPPORTED EMPLOYMENT GUIDING PRINCIPLES	OTHER TYPES OF EMPLOYMENT SERVICES
7. Job supports are offered to working people on a continuous basis. Job supports are services that help a person succeed on the job. The IPS team provides long-term supports (on average, one year). Afterward, mental health practitioners, such as case managers, provide ongoing supports to people who have been working successfully for a significant period of time. **Rationale:** The amount of job supports people need may increase or decrease over time depending on their symptoms of mental illness or other issues in their lives.	Many programs offer job supports on a time-limited basis, for example, ninety days after finding work.

You may have concerns that if your family member does not do well at a job, he or she will be faced with another failure. In IPS, each job is viewed as a positive learning experience. For example, if a person loses a job because he or she is late for work each morning, the employment specialist might talk to the person about whether or not to provide wake-up calls for the next job or just look for an afternoon or evening job. Further, IPS specialists provide supports to people who are working. Sometimes, they provide supports right on the job. For example, they may go to work with the person to help him or her learn the job. Frequently, employment specialists provide supports off the job. For example, they may meet with the person to talk about the job, help learn the bus route, or help review an orientation manual. With permission from the person who is working, employment specialists can also talk to employers to get extra feedback to share with the worker.

You may also have concerns that your family member will risk losing his or her benefits, particularly medical benefits. The majority of people who receive Social Security or other benefits are able to work without losing medical benefits, if that is their preference. IPS programs offer access to benefits planning with trained benefits counselors. Family members can ask to sit in on these meetings, so they can learn more about work incentives that allow people to work while retaining part or all of their benefits.

State Vocational Rehabilitation

Each state, as well as the District of Columbia and U.S. territories, supports a division of vocational rehabilitation (VR) that has offices throughout the state to provide vocational rehabilitation services for individuals with disabilities. Rehabilitation counselors at these offices sometimes provide direct services to clients, but more often contract with local programs (such as IPS supported employment programs) to provide assistance with employment. When a program, such as IPS, is providing side-by-side assistance to the person who wants to work, the rehabilitation counselor helps develop the employment plan and stays in touch with the employment specialist and client to share vocational expertise. The VR counselor may also be able to help with resources such as bus passes or work clothes, but that type of assistance varies from person to person and depends on the person's employment plan.

When IPS programs work collaboratively with vocational rehabilitation, the IPS program encourages the vocational rehabilitation counselor to provide services in a manner that is consistent with the IPS approach. For example, the VR counselor would not ask people to complete vocational evaluations or trial jobs to demonstrate that they are ready to work. Further, while rehabilitation counselors may need to close cases after ninety days of employment, IPS programs continue to provide job supports for as long as the worker wants and needs the assistance— on average, about one year. Although your family member may have tried VR without success in the past, we've found that people who participate in both services simultaneously do better than those who only participate in one service or the other. Rehabilitation counselors report that they appreciate the intensity of services provided by the IPS team and mental health practitioners. And IPS programs benefit from VR counselor's knowledge of the local job market, secondary disabilities, resources, and so forth.

Family Involvement in IPS Supported Employment

Families can play an important role in the person's employment plan. For example, family members may have information about the person's previous jobs and education experiences. They may also know about the person's illness and strategies to manage symptoms. Families often know the person so well that they can suggest good job matches. Unfortunately, many employment specialists do not reach out to family members and include them in meetings with the client. Helping employment specialists learn how to connect with families is an important role of IPS supervisors. Ask your family member if he or she would like you to participate in some meetings about his or her employment plan. If your family member is comfortable with that, the two of you could call the employment specialist to schedule a meeting. The employment specialist and VR counselor will only be able to meet with you if they also talk to your family member and obtain permission.

Examples of participation from family members:

A father in Ohio met with his son and an employment specialist to talk about his son's efforts to work. The father had been discouraged that his son was working only five hours per week until he learned that his son was struggling with symptoms on the job. He was also glad to learn that his son's plan was to gradually increase his work hours once he was comfortable with the job.

■ ■ ■

A brother in Oregon met with his sister, her employment specialist, and her VR counselor to talk about his sister's desire to work. He had been close to his sister for many years and was able to share information about her previous jobs—things that went well and situations that didn't work out. For example, he knew that his sister would need help getting to the job in the morning and that she hadn't done well on jobs that involved doing multiple tasks at once. This information helped his sister and employment specialist think of jobs that would be a good match.

■ ■ ■

A woman in Chicago reported that she had been on the verge of losing her job because she was becoming psychotic. She said that she didn't believe she needed medication, even when her treatment team suggested that she resume taking her medication. However, after her case manager, employment specialist, and pastor met with her, she decided to go back on medication. In hindsight, she was happy with that decision and reported that her pastor had been the person who was able to help her make the choice to take medications.

A mother met with her daughter and employment specialist to talk about possible jobs. She knew a manager who hired people for the types of jobs her daughter wanted and helped the employment specialist make a connection to that person.

■ ■ ■

After meeting with his wife and her employment specialist, a husband made a point of occasionally telling his wife that he was proud of her efforts to work.

■ ■ ■

A daughter met with her mother and a benefits planner to find out how her mother's Social Security benefits would be affected by a return to work. She agreed to help her mother keep track of her earnings and report her pay to the Social Security Administration.

Don't let the employment plan become a source of conflict for your family. Also, try to avoid meetings with the employment specialist unless your family member is present. You wouldn't want your family member to feel that you were talking about him or her behind his or her back. IPS programs should empower the person to listen to suggestions and encouragement from others, but to ultimately be the one to make decisions for his or her own life.

Also, if you have concerns about your family member returning to work, we urge you to meet with the employment specialist and your family member to talk about those concerns. The employment specialist will ultimately follow your family member's wishes, even when those differ from your own. However, any information you share may still help your family member. And keeping the lines of communication open may lead to collaboration over time.

Finding IPS Supported Employment Programs
IPS supported employment programs are not yet available in all areas. If you reside in the United States, we suggest that you contact your state department of mental health to ask whether an IPS program exists in your area: www.cdc.gov/mentalhealth/state_orgs.htm. Also, be aware that many employment programs use the title *supported employment.* In many cases, the title does not refer to the practice described in this chapter. Be sure to ask if the program is "Individual Placement and Support (IPS) supported employment" and also ask if

the program is using the Supported Employment Fidelity Scale that was updated in 2008. (The Fidelity Scale ensures that the program is following the carefully researched, recommended procedures.) If not, it is likely to be another type of program.

Once you find a program, we hope the services are delivered as described in this chapter. If not, talk to the employment specialist (and possibly his or her supervisor) about any discrepancies you observe. If this is not satisfactory, you may wish to call the clinical director of mental health services to ask about the steps that the program is taking to implement IPS according to the fidelity scale. You may even ask if the agency has a steering committee or an IPS leadership team that includes family members so that you can participate in discussions about program implementation. For more about steering committees, see page 221.

If you are unable to locate an IPS program in your area, you may wish to contact your state department of Vocational Rehabilitation to learn about other employment programs for your family member. To find your state office of Vocational Rehabilitation, go to http://askjan.org. Select "Job Seekers." Scroll down to "Federal, State, and Local Resources," and click on it. Scroll down to "Vocational Rehabilitation Agencies (VR)."

Advocacy for IPS Supported Employment

NAMI (National Alliance on Mental Illness) is an advocacy organization with state chapters and national leadership. Family members, people with mental illnesses, and others can join NAMI to obtain education about mental illness, to advocate for better laws affecting people with mental illnesses, to advocate for better treatment and more research on mental illnesses, and to fight stigma against people with mental illnesses. Many NAMI state and local chapters are endorsing IPS supported employment. Contact your local or state NAMI office to find out if you can help with advocacy efforts. (Find your NAMI by going to www.nami.org. Then click on "Find Your Local NAMI.")

You can also help by talking to legislators about the importance of work for people with severe mental illnesses. Some talking points might include the following:

- Tell them how work has helped a person you know who has mental illness.

- Let them know that research has demonstrated that 60–80 percent of people with severe mental illnesses want to work, but that only 11–15 percent of people with severe mental illnesses are employed.

- Explain that money is spent every year on employment programs of various types, but that research shows that IPS is the most effective approach to help people with jobs.

- Share brief educational materials with legislators. Check the end of this chapter to find out how to obtain advocacy materials.

Finally, talk to your state department of mental health and local mental health centers about IPS supported employment. Ask them if they have heard about the evidence-based approach for helping people with jobs and refer them to the following Web site to learn more: http://www.dartmouth.edu/~ips.

SUMMARY

IPS supported employment is a particular type of employment program that is well researched and carefully defined. IPS programs that follow specific practices and achieve high fidelity using the Supported Employment Fidelity Scale (the content of which was revised in 2008) are more likely to help people obtain community jobs. With permission from their family member, families can participate in IPS by meeting with the employment specialist, their family member, and possibly a VR counselor and/or case manager to talk about the employment plan. Family members can share helpful information about the person, encourage the person's efforts, and help celebrate successes. Finally, family members who are interested in advocacy for IPS supported employment can contact their state department of mental health or offer to participate in local steering committees for IPS. They might also contact state and local NAMI offices to talk about IPS supported employment.

I feel that employment is critical to help my son cope better in society. Next to a cure for his illness, work has as much impact as anything.

—Ed

TOOLS FOR FAMILIES WHO WISH TO LEARN ABOUT, OR ADVOCATE FOR, IPS SUPPORTED EMPLOYMENT:

- Summer 2008 Supported Employment newsletter: Focus on Families. www.dartmouth.edu/~ips. Select "Free Newsletter." Select "Previous Newsletters," then "Summer 2008."

- IPS Supported Employment advocacy brochure. Go to www.dartmouth.edu/~ips. Select "Resources." Select "Brochures," then "Advocacy Handout." Request copies by using the ordering information on the Web site.

- Ask questions about IPS supported employment by going to http://www.dartmouth.edu/~ips. Select "ASK about IPS." Submit your questions about IPS.

- We recommend the videos *3 Faces, 3 Lives* and *Introduction English* or *Introduction Spanish* to hear first-person accounts of using IPS supported employment services. Go to www.dartmouth.edu/~ips. Select "Resources," then "Videos." Select "Introducing IPS Supported Employment." Select "3 Faces, 3 Lives" or "Introduction English" (or "Introduction Spanish").

▼

CONCLUSION

Some people worry that evidence-based practices are not individualized. This perception indicates lack of knowledge about how IPS works. IPS supported employment requires practitioners and supervisors to develop specific skills to be applied in different ways for each individual client. Think about the client interviewing skills that we described in the third chapter. Many of those skills do not come naturally and must be practiced. Further, many of the principles of IPS supported employment require a high degree of creativity. Practitioners must be able to understand the needs of each client and think of multiple solutions to problems in order to provide individualized job development and follow-along supports. IPS supported employment requires a thoughtful approach in which practitioners learn about each person's strengths and then anticipate areas in which the person may need help. Practitioners must be open to new information as the person tries jobs and be willing to change the plan as needed.

Effective practitioners take time to understand what is important to each client. Practitioners who are knowledgeable about job finding and career development may sometimes be tempted to lead clients in one direction or another. But the steps that someone takes to build a working life can only be his or her own. There are times when practitioners must slow down to try doing things the client's way and must suspend their disbelief that a certain strategy will work.

Helping people with work requires a team approach. Case managers, substance abuse counselors, medication prescribers, rehabilitation counselors from VR, employment specialists, housing staff, clients, and in some cases, family members, each have their own perspective and specialized contributions to make. Employment specialists cannot be effective without the help of a multidisciplinary team. Team members can help with issues related to the person's symptoms, personal life, or substance use and may even supply the occasional job lead.

It's important for all of us to be open to change. IPS supported employment is an evolving practice. As we continue to learn more about how to help people succeed at work, the practice will continue to evolve. Some areas that we are learning about now include career development, effective job development services for people

Duplicating this page is illegal. Do not copy this material without written permission from the publisher.

217

with criminal justice system involvement, specific techniques that VR counselors can use when working with IPS supported employment, peer-operated agencies that provide IPS supported employment programs, and supported employment and education for young adults who have recently been diagnosed with mental illness.

Finally, the mental health and vocational rehabilitation fields should never minimize the importance of helping with work. People who are recovering from severe mental illnesses report that work can change the way they think about themselves and even change how they live. Below, Ted shares his feelings about how work helped him with recovery:

▫ ◼ ▫

I've had mental illness now for about twenty-five years. That's a really long time. It started when I had just graduated from college and was going to go to graduate school or get a job near the ocean. I had so much to look forward to. It was so disappointing to feel that things were nipped in the bud. At first I just wanted to go home to my parents and avoid the world. I felt detached and lethargic. It was a very heavy-duty sort of thing. But I finally decided that I needed to make a life for myself whether I had a mental illness or not. I decided that I needed to go to work so that I could feel more self-reliant.

Having a job has been tremendously helpful to me. Empowering. I feel like a healthier person. I feel comfortable with the rhythms of work and the ins and outs of work. I'm working full time now and I've just been awarded some money to take a college course. I'm lucky because now I'm at a point where I want to forge ahead. I feel like myself again.

APPENDIX

IPS SUPPORTED EMPLOYMENT FIDELITY

I have found fidelity reviews to be helpful. The reviewers assisted us in identifying the things we were doing well and the things we needed to improve. Fidelity reviews helped us figure out where we were with implementation. The reports also included concrete recommendations to help us think about how to move forward. The recommendations ultimately helped us improve our outcomes.

At one point, my agency took a look at the scale and tried to score our own program, but it was difficult for us to be objective. We thought we were doing better than we actually were. Later on, we had a fidelity review conducted by outside reviewers, and when we read the report, we began to understand how to interpret the scale. It helped us gain a better understanding of what IPS supported employment is really about.

We continue to invite reviewers to our agency on an annual basis. I think the key is to keep an open mind about the review and be willing to try the recommendations. Fidelity reviews are just a great quality improvement tool.

—Ginger Yanchar, IPS Supervisor

Fidelity refers to the degree that a particular program follows the standards for an evidence-based practice. A *fidelity scale* is a tool to measure the quality of implementation of an evidence-based practice. The Supported Employment Fidelity Scale defines the critical ingredients of IPS supported employment in order to help programs identify areas to celebrate and areas to improve. When not being used for research, fidelity scales are simply a quality improvement tool, a way to help programs improve outcomes. As demonstrated through research, high-fidelity programs have better employment outcomes than low-fidelity programs.

The Supported Employment Fidelity Scale is divided into three sections, including *staffing, organization,* and *services*. Within each major category are subsections. For example, under staffing, fidelity is examined by caseload size and the focus and duties of the employment services staff. Each item is rated on a five-point response format, ranging from 1 = no implementation to 5 = full implementation, with intermediate numbers representing progressively greater degrees of implementation. The score sheet has four categories: not IPS, fair fidelity, good fidelity, and exemplary fidelity. To view the scale and score sheet, see the CD-ROM.

Looking at the fidelity scale may provide some guidelines for improving program fidelity at your agency. The scale may stimulate practitioners, supervisors, and administrators to discuss current services and ways to improve those services. An agency work group might discuss how other vocational programs, for instance, a work adjustment program, affect items such as "ongoing work-based assessment" or "rapid job search."

Many individuals have difficulty interpreting the scale for their own agencies, as the program administrator at the beginning of this chapter pointed out. To obtain accurate fidelity assessments, agencies should work with people trained in the use of the fidelity scale. Such fidelity reviewers usually visit agencies for two days to interview staff, talk to clients, observe practitioners at work, sit in on meetings, go out with employment specialists to contact employers, and read a sample of client records. The fidelity reviewers then prepare a report that includes a score for each item, an explanation of each score, and recommendations to improve fidelity.

Some states have developed fidelity review teams that provide this service to agencies. If your state doesn't have a trained fidelity review team, think about other ways to use the fidelity scale. For example, people who are not closely connected to the IPS team, such as quality assurance managers, might read the fidelity manual available for download at www.dartmouth.edu/~ips. Select

"Fidelity." Select "SE Fidelity Manual." Next, they might schedule a fidelity visit with the team. When in doubt about how to apply the scale, reviewers can submit their questions online for the Dartmouth IPS Supported Employment Team to answer. To do this, go to the Web site above. Select "ASK about IPS."

We recommend that agencies use fidelity reviews not as a report card, but as a quality improvement tool. For example, agencies that successfully implement IPS supported employment develop a written plan to improve fidelity items with low scores. The fidelity plan includes specific information about action steps, individuals responsible, and target dates. Further, these agencies often chart fidelity scores over time so that they have a clear picture of program improvement and can target areas that seem to stagnate or decrease in fidelity. For example:

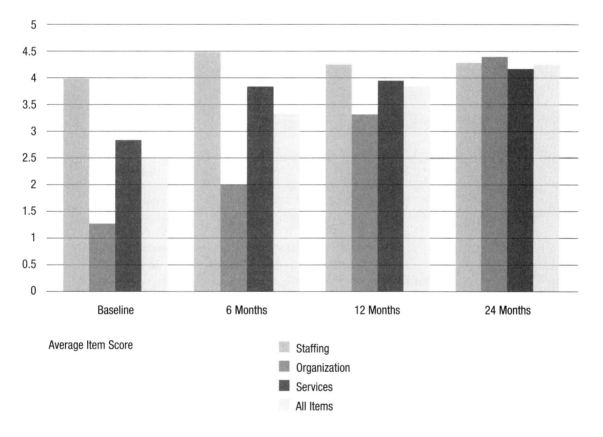

Sample IPS Fidelity Scores

Steering committees can help agencies achieve better implementation. Internal steering committees include agency personnel, the clinical director, the IPS supervisor, and the chief operating officer or quality assurance director. This team understands how the agency works and has the authority to make changes.

Typically, internal steering committees meet monthly until good fidelity is achieved, and then might meet a few times after each fidelity review. External steering committees include some agency personnel along with outside stakeholders such as VR counselors, clients, family members, local college or training program representatives, and others. External steering committees usually meet quarterly to help the agency staff consider ways to expand the program, reach out to clients who are not employed, and improve fidelity. For more information about steering committees, see IPS Supported Employment Steering Committees on the CD-ROM.

Even when agencies have bright, motivated, and experienced staff, they can improve with help from an objective expert. Fidelity assessments provide a road map to help agency staff ensure that they are providing services based on the well-researched approach of IPS supported employment.

• • •

TOOLS FOR USING IPS SUPPORTED EMPLOYMENT FIDELITY SCALE:

Supported Employment Fidelity Scale (content revised January 2008)

Sample IPS Supported Employment Fidelity Action Plan

● IPS Supported Employment Fidelity Manual (provides information about how to interpret fidelity items) can be downloaded from www.dartmouth.edu/~ips. Select "Fidelity." Select "SE Fidelity Manual."

IPS Supported Employment Steering Committees

Early Implementation IPS Supported Employment Steering Committee Sample Meeting Agenda

Sample IPS Supported Employment Fidelity Report

APPENDIX

FORMS AND HANDOUTS ON THE CD-ROM

The resources that are also available in Spanish have this icon (SP) next to them.

Part I. IPS Supported Employment Fidelity

1. Supported Employment Fidelity Scale (content revised in 2008)

2. Supported Employment Fidelity Scale Score Sheet

3. Sample IPS Supported Employment Fidelity Action Plan

4. Sample IPS Supported Employment Fidelity Report

Part II. IPS Supported Employment Tools

5. Family Members: What You Need to Know about IPS Supported Employment (handout version of chapter 13 for family members) (SP)

6. Plan for Approaching Employers/Disclosure Worksheet (SP)

7. Career Profile Face Sheet/IPS Supported Employment Referral (SP)

8. Career Profile (SP)

9. Job Start Report

10. Job Ending Report

11. Education Experience Report

12. Employer Contact Log

13. Sample Employer Contact Log

14. Sample Employer Thank-You Letter

15. Sample Employer Thank-You Note

16. IPS Supervisor's Guide to Individualized Follow-Along Plans

17. Sample Job Follow-Along Plan

18. Sample Education Support Plan

19. Information Sheet: Employment Supports for Clients with Co-occurring Mental Illnesses and Substance Use Disorders (SP)

20. Strategies for Collaboration between IPS Supported Employment Programs and State Vocational Rehabilitation

21. Sample Employment Specialist Job Description

22. Sample IPS Supported Employment Supervisor Job Description

23. Field Mentoring Log for Job Development

24. Field Mentoring Log for Skills Development

25. IPS Supported Employment Supervision Record

26. Employment Specialist Orientation Checklist

27. "So, you may be interested in a job . . ." Worksheet (SP)

28. IPS Supported Employment Steering Committees

29. Early Implementation IPS Supported Employment Steering Committee Sample Meeting Agenda

30. Sustaining IPS Supported Employment Program Steering Committee Sample Meeting Agenda

• • •

▼

SUGGESTED READING

IPS Supported Employment

Becker, D. R., and R. E. Drake. *A Working Life for People with Severe Mental Illness.* New York: Oxford University Press, 2003.

Becker, D. R., R. Whitley, E. L. Bailey, and R. E. Drake. "Long-Term Employment Trajectories among Supported Employment Participants with Severe Mental Illness." *Psychiatric Services* 58 (2007): 922–28.

Dartmouth Psychiatric Research Center has materials online that may be downloaded without cost. For example, the demonstration videos referenced in the chapters, newsletters, and fidelity information. See www.dartmouth.edu/~ips.

Supported Employment Implementation Resource Kit. http://mentalhealth.samhsa.gov/cmhs/communitysupport/toolkits/employment/default.asp.

Co-occurring Disorders and IPS Supported Employment

Becker, D. R., R. E. Drake, and W. J. Naughton. "Supported Employment for People with Co-occurring Disorders." *Psychiatric Rehabilitation Journal* 28, no. 4 (2005): 332–38.

Motivational Interviewing

Miller, W. R., and S. Rollnick. *Motivational Interviewing: Preparing People for Change.* New York: Guilford Press, 2002.

Web site: www.motivationalinterview.org

Strengths-Based Services

Rapp, C. A., and R. J. Goscha. *The Strengths Model: Case Management with People with Psychiatric Disabilities.* New York: Oxford University Press, 2006.

Duplicating this page is illegal. Do not copy this material without written permission from the publisher.

225

▼

REFERENCES

Becker, D. R., G. R. Bond, D. McCarthy, D. Thompson, H. Xie, G. J. McHugo, et al. 2001. Converting day treatment centers to supported employment programs in Rhode Island. *Psychiatric Services* 52:351–57.

Becker, D. R., and R. E. Drake. 1994. Individual placement and support: A community mental health center approach to vocational rehabilitation. *Community Mental Health Journal* 30:193–205.

Becker, D. R., and R. E. Drake. 2003. *A working life for people with severe mental illness.* New York: Oxford University Press.

Becker, D. R., R. E. Drake, A. Farabaugh, and G. R. Bond. 1996. Job preferences of clients with severe psychiatric disorders participating in supported employment programs. *Psychiatric Services* 47:1223–26.

Becker, D. R., R. E. Drake, and W. Naughton. 2005. Supported employment for people with co-occurring disorders. *Psychiatric Rehabilitation Journal* 28:332–38.

Bissonnctte, D. 1994. *Beyond traditional job development: The art of creating opportunity.* Chatsworth, CA: Milt Wright and Associates.

Bond, G. R. 2004. Supported employment: Evidence for an evidence-based practice. *Psychiatric Rehabilitation Journal* 27:345–59.

Bond, G. R., D. R. Becker, R. E. Drake, and K. M. Vogler. 1997. A fidelity scale for the individual placement and support model of supported employment. *Rehabilitation Counseling Bulletin* 40:265–84.

Bond, G. R., R. E. Drake, and D. R. Becker. 2008. An update on randomized controlled trials of evidence-based supported employment. *Psychiatric Rehabilitation Journal* 31:280–90.

Clark, R. E., H. Xie, D. R. Becker, and R. E. Drake. 1998. Benefits and costs of supported employment from three perspectives. *Journal of Behavioral Health Services and Research* 25:22–34.

Egan, G. 1986. *The skilled helper.* 3rd ed. Monterey: Brooks/Cole.

Duplicating this page is illegal. Do not copy this material without written permission from the publisher.

227

MacDonald-Wilson, K. L., E. S. Rogers, J. M. Massaro, A. Lyass, and T. Crean. 2002. An investigation of reasonable workplace accommodations for people with psychiatric disabilities: Quantitative findings from a multi-site study. *Community Mental Health Journal* 38:35–50.

McGurk, S. R., and K. Mueser. 2006. Strategies for coping with cognitive impairments of clients in supported employment. *Psychiatric Services* 57:1421–29.

Miller, W. R., and S. Rollnick. 2002. *Motivational interviewing: Preparing people for change.* 2nd ed. New York: Guilford Press.

Mueser, K. T., D. R. Becker, and R. Wolfe. 2001. Supported employment, job preferences, and job tenure and satisfaction. *Journal of Mental Health* 10:411–17.

Nuechterlein, K. H., K. L. Subotnick, L. R. Turner, and J. Ventura. 2008. Individual placement and support for individuals with recent-onset schizophrenia: Integrating supported education and supported employment. *Psychiatric Rehabilitation Journal* 31:340–49.

Ticket to Work Program Evaluation Committee. 2001. *Report and recommendations.* Columbus, OH: Ohio Senate, 5. (Online at http://www.lsc.state.oh.us/legreports/ttwp.pdf.)

ABOUT THE AUTHORS

Sarah J. Swanson, L.S.W., C.R.C., is a supported employment trainer for Dartmouth Psychiatric Research Center. She received her bachelor's degree in Vocational Rehabilitation Counseling and her master's in Rehabilitation Psychology from the University of Wisconsin–Madison. Recently Ms. Swanson was the director of Supported Employment Training for the Ohio Supported Employment CCOE. She also has sixteen years of experience in community mental health systems.

Deborah R. Becker, M.Ed., C.R.C., is associate professor of Community and Family Medicine and of Psychiatry at Dartmouth Medical School. She has been a rehabilitation specialist at Dartmouth Psychiatric Research Center for twenty years. Ms. Becker has been project director for vocational, housing, and dual diagnosis research studies. She has described and researched the Individual Placement and Support approach to supported employment. She codeveloped the SAMHSA Evidence-Based Practice Supported Employment Implementation Resource Kit. She is codirector of the Johnson and Johnson collaborative that is organized to improve access to evidence-based supported employment in thirteen states. She has written extensively in the area of vocational rehabilitation. She provides consultation and training on vocational rehabilitation and program implementation. Ms. Becker has also worked in the positions of direct service and administration in community support programs for people with serious mental illness.

Duplicating this page is illegal. Do not copy this material without written permission from the publisher.

229